Envisioning a Comprehensive Peace Agreement for Afghanistan

LAUREL E. MILLER, JONATHAN S. BLAKE

RAND NATIONAL SECURITY RESEARCH DIVISION

For more information on this publication, visit www.rand.org/t/RR2937

Library of Congress Cataloging-in-Publication Data is available for this publication.
ISBN: 978-1-9774-0407-7

Published by the RAND Corporation, Santa Monica, Calif.

Preface

In this report, we paint a detailed picture of a plausible final comprehensive peace agreement for Afghanistan. The report includes analysis of realistic compromises, presented in the form of a complete peace agreement text. The authors produced the text on the basis of research on the interests and views of the conflict parties, comparative research on past peace agreements from around the world, and extensive consultations with officials, former officials, and experts associated with all the parties and with other interested governments. The work is intended to provide a source of concrete ideas regarding potential outcomes of a peace process for use by conflict party negotiators and others interested in encouraging a negotiated settlement of the war in Afghanistan.

This research was sponsored by the government of a U.S. ally and conducted within the International Security and Defense Policy Center of the RAND National Security Research Division (NSRD). NSRD conducts research and analysis for the Office of the Secretary of Defense, the Joint Staff, the Unified Combatant Commands, the defense agencies, the Navy, the Marine Corps, the U.S. Coast Guard, the U.S. Intelligence Community, allied foreign governments, and foundations.

For more information on the RAND International Security and Defense Policy Center, see www.rand.org/nsrd/ndri/centers/isdp or contact the center director (contact information is provided on the webpage).

Contents

Summary

Despite years of halting attempts to begin negotiating an end to the war in Afghanistan, none of the conflict parties has articulated more than the barest outlines of envisioned outcomes of a negotiation. Even as the prospects of a peace process gaining traction rose during 2019, the parties' visions of a political settlement remained obscure and underdeveloped. This lack of detailed analysis and policy spelling out the issues likely to arise in a peace process and proposing potential substantive solutions has been one of many obstacles to moving a process forward. Overcoming resistance on the part of conflict actors who have long been invested in prosecution of the war, or who fear what compromise with the enemy might bring, is made more difficult by the absence of depiction of a plausible political settlement. The purpose of the work presented in this report is to paint such a picture for policymakers on all sides of the conflict and for others interested in encouraging negotiations.

To show concretely what the outcome of negotiations could look like, we chose to write a peace agreement rather than write about one. That is, we translated our research and analysis into the format of a comprehensive peace accord. Our intention is not to present this document as a model agreement in a normative sense; we do not claim that the draft agreement represents a set of purported international best practices. Nor does the document represent the authors' judgments about the most desirable terms for an Afghan peace agreement. Rather, our intent is to lay out plausible compromises on the issues likely to be most important, in a form that would stand some chance of actually being implemented. The result, therefore, does not reflect any one conflict party's preferred set of solutions. We hope this approach will help the parties envision a final peace agreement and develop realistic negotiating positions toward that end.

Methodology

Our research involved three types of sources: (1) published material describing the interests and probable goals of the conflict parties related to a potential peace process, (2) past peace agreements, both for Afghanistan and for many other countries around the world, and (3) in-person confidential consultations, primarily during the second half of 2018, with approximately 85 individuals. Those consulted include people associated in their current or former positions with all sides of the conflict and with states neighboring Afghanistan, as well as experts on Afghanistan and peace processes. In our comparative research, rather than looking for past peace agreements that more or less in totality could serve as models for Afghanistan, we took a cross-cutting, thematic approach. After identifying issues likely to arise in an Afghan peace process, we searched past peace agreements for examples of how similar issues have been addressed. We also used our review of peace agreements to identify additional issues to address in our peace agreement. Instead of looking for blueprints, we treated the past agreements as sources of ideas and inspiration for substance, format, and specific wording.

The Agreement

Although we crafted our agreement text as a comprehensive political settlement, portions of the text could potentially be used in separate agreements in a phased manner, if advantageous for achieving negotiating progress. However, the most important issues might be seen by one or more parties as too interdependent to separate into phased agreements. In footnotes to the text, we offer alternative options for the most difficult issues. The **structure** comprises

- an Agreement on a Comprehensive Settlement, with Parts I and III including commitments by four parties (Afghan government, Taliban, United States, and North Atlantic Treaty Organization [NATO]) and Part II including commitments of two parties (Taliban and Afghan government)
- an agreement between Afghanistan and Pakistan that would be signed simultaneously with the main Comprehensive Settlement
- a Declaration by supporting states that also would be signed simultaneously with the main Comprehensive Settlement.

Negotiators might want to include, as an additional document, a side agreement among the important pro-government Afghan political parties and factions stating that the Afghan government's signature on the agreement represents the assent of all these groups. Drafting such a side agreement early in the process might help defuse persistent disputes over what would constitute a sufficiently representative negotiating team on the anti-Taliban side.

The main elements of the Agreement on a Comprehensive Settlement are summarized below, without the alternative options offered in Chapter Three.

- A **core bargain** involving both the internal and external parties that includes
  - a comprehensive ceasefire and cessation of hostilities
  - a complete renunciation by the Taliban of links with international terrorist groups
  - a complete, phased ending of the current U.S./NATO military mission over an 18-month (but extendable) transitional time period, based on completion of agreement implementation milestones
  - an invitation by the Afghan parties to the international community to form a small, limited "Afghanistan Support Team" focused exclusively on counterterrorism action and assistance,

especially against the Islamic State in Iraq and Syria–Khorasan Province, coupled with a request for a named country (determined during negotiations) to organize the team
  - the expressed intention of the United States to continue providing civilian assistance and to solicit contributions from other donors.
- New **political arrangements** within Afghanistan that include
  - inclusivity and broad-based representation as the fundamental guiding principles
  - a process for the adoption of a new constitution within 12 months, with some elements and principles for the new constitution included in the agreement text
  - the 2004 Constitution remaining in effect until adoption of a new constitution, except where inconsistent with the agreement (the process specified in the agreement for adopting a new constitution would be followed instead of the amendment procedures in the 2004 Constitution)
  - a presidential system, with somewhat reduced powers for the president and increased balancing of presidential power compared with the current system
  - a modest degree of devolution of authority to the provincial level of government to promote broad distribution of power among demographic and political groups in areas where they are concentrated and to recalibrate the center-regions relationship (not a shift to federalism, but a shift toward more opportunities for a greater number of political and demographic groups to exercise a share of governmental power)
  - flexibility for governance arrangements at the district level, to create space for localized solutions
  - the establishment of a High Council of Islamic Scholars with roles in evaluating the consistency of legislation with Islamic tenets and principles and in advising the government.
- Establishment of a **Transitional Government** for the 18-month transition period, including a Transitional Executive with a negotiated by-name list of a Chairman, several Vice Chairmen, and members (rotating chairmanship is suggested as an inferior alter-

native in case the parties cannot agree on a single individual to serve as Chairman).

- **Security arrangements** that include
  - reconstitution of the armed forces to make leadership more inclusive and broadly representative of the population and to provide equitable opportunity for inclusion among the rank and file
  - a single national army, air force, border police, and intelligence service
  - devolution of policing responsibility to the provincial level
  - prohibition of armed groups not explicitly authorized by the state, once reconstitution is completed
  - disarmament only of heavy weapons.
- **Transitional security** arrangements until reconstitution that include
  - forces of each side responsible for security and public order in areas over which they exercise control, in accordance with a negotiated map of areas of responsibility
  - the establishment of a Joint Military Commission with duties including coordinating across areas of responsibility and establishing a joint command structure.
- Broad **amnesty**, consistent with Afghan precedent, balanced with creating a process for promoting **reconciliation**.
- Release of all conflict-related **prisoners/detainees**, based on a negotiated list of persons to be released.
- Request for international assistance with the **return of refugees** and displaced persons.
- Establishment of a process for addressing **land and property** disputes.
- Request for establishment of a **Monitoring and Verification Team** under the "good offices" of the United Nations Secretary-General.
- Removal of all remaining **sanctions** imposed on members of the Taliban in connection with their membership in or activities related to the Taliban, except for any persons who reject the agreement.

- Establishment of a **Joint Implementation Commission** composed of the parties to the agreement, responsible for resolving any disputes over interpretation of the agreement. (If a neutral facilitating or mediating body or state becomes involved in the negotiating process, or if circumstances change to make a peacekeeping body or guarantor become plausible, this Commission should include such a neutral actor. Without a neutral actor involved, the risk is higher that the Commission might not function effectively.)

The text does not include a request for a peacekeeping mission to be organized by or a ceasefire guarantor role to be played by a neutral organization or state. This gap raises the risk of implementation failure but reflects the current lack of appetite within the international community for potentially taking on such responsibilities.

Because the conflict parties have developed their specific negotiating aims, positions, and acceptable fall-back options only to a limited extent, as of this report's publication, it is difficult to assess with certainty how well our proposed agreement text meets their goals and avoids crossing their redlines. The text in its entirety is not likely to meet with the ready approval of any party because—as a real peace agreement will need to be—it is a compromise document, both in terms of specific provisions and of balancing among provisions.

Nevertheless, several elements of the text would likely appeal to the parties in important respects:

- **For the pro-government side**, the main contours of the post-2001 democratic political system are left intact. The existing constitution is maintained as the starting point for revisions and stays in effect until a new document is put in place. Continued support from the United States and other donors is anticipated.
- **For the Taliban**, the presence of U.S. and NATO forces is brought to an end. An opportunity is created for adopting a fresh constitution. A High Council of Islamic Scholars is introduced into the system of government, which could be a vehicle for real-

izing aspects of Islamic governance. And sanctions removal is provided, thus signifying the political legitimization of the Taliban.
- **For the United States**, there are counter-terrorism assurances, and there is a pathway toward ending its military involvement in Afghanistan in a manner that has some prospect of leaving stability in its wake.

In some respects, crafting compromises required skating close to potential redlines; whether some of the proposals cross such lines depends on how the parties' positions evolve during negotiations. Elements of particular note in this regard include the following:

- The request for foreign security cooperation and assistance focused on counterterrorism might not be acceptable to the Taliban because it would authorize the continued presence of some foreign forces, even though the provision is written in a way intended to maximize acceptability.
- The modest degree of devolution of authority from the central to provincial level proposed in our agreement would not be the first choice of the Taliban or some of the factions on the pro-government side but might be a satisfactory second choice, if they see during negotiations that there are not enough assured shares of power to spread around otherwise. We cannot be sure, however, that even our quite limited proposal would not be rejected out of hand by ethnic Pashtuns in particular, for whom any suggestion of decentralization has been controversial until now. (Political representatives of minority ethnic groups have tended to favor some forms of decentralization.)
- The proposal to somewhat reduce the current system's extraordinary scope of presidential power might not be attractive to either the government or the Taliban (assuming the Taliban are prepared to entertain the idea of an elected president), given the insistence of both on a highly centralized system. However, it is difficult to envisage how to resolve opposing interests in gaining hold of maximal power without lessening the winner-take-all nature of the existing presidential system.

- Our agreement identifies the government of the Islamic Republic of Afghanistan and the Islamic Movement of the Afghan Taliban as parties and signatories. As of this writing, the Taliban had not agreed to negotiate with the government as such and had not agreed to give up use of the name "Islamic Emirate of Afghanistan." Reference to the "Emirate" is a probable redline for the pro-government side. Alternatives such as signature by the negotiators individually or no signatures at all might be feasible but would be more appropriate for a peace agreement in a situation of complete rupture from the preceding regime rather than conditions requiring mutual accommodation of opposing parties.

Key Implementation Risks

Any peace agreement in Afghanistan, no matter how closely it does or does not resemble the agreement we present, will be vulnerable to implementation failure. Peace implementation processes following intense and protracted conflict understandably tend to be fraught in general; the research and analysis undertaken for this report illuminated several specific high-probability risks for Afghanistan in particular.

Power-Sharing Could Exacerbate Afghanistan's Political Fragility

Over the last two decades, Afghan politics even without involvement of the Taliban have been fractious, political stability has been fragile, and competition for resources (in a patronage-based system) has been intense. Institutions are still weak and therefore provide little ballast for the ship of state. Introducing the Taliban into this picture in any sort of power-sharing arrangement is not likely to quickly bring greater stability. Indeed, drawing the largely Pashtun Taliban into the political mainstream could introduce another political fault line, among Pashtuns. Forceful Afghan leadership and strong external support will be needed to overcome the naturally dim prospects of reaching a political settlement that is so clear and uncontested in its terms that its implementation is not threatened by chronic political instability and power struggles.

Clear-Enough Transitional Security Arrangements Will Be Tough to Achieve

One of the most difficult elements to negotiate and perhaps the area of greatest implementation vulnerability will be security arrangements for the immediate aftermath of a peace agreement, regardless of whether the parties adopt a comprehensive or phased approach to concluding an agreement. If the negotiating parties and their soldiers and fighters do not have clear understandings of who is authorized to use force and where they are authorized to use it during the implementation period, any agreement could quickly unravel as a result of escalation of local disputes, purposeful spoiling, or other reasons for outbreaks of violence.

Implementation Probably Will Not Be Guaranteed by a Peacekeeping or Peace Enforcement Mission

Another significant vulnerability is likely to be the lack of a peacekeeping or peace enforcement mission to guarantee implementation of an agreement. There is as yet no evidence of international appetite for such a mission. The main external mechanism for enforcement will therefore be threat of reintervention, but after nearly 20 years of foreign military intervention in Afghanistan, the political bar for reinsertion of forces at least on the part of the United States and NATO will likely be quite high. Political support for an agreement on the part of regional powers and international financial support could somewhat mitigate the lack of a hard-power guarantee of implementation. Robust cooperation among the regional powers in common support of Afghanistan's stability—although not impossible—would be historically anomalous, however. The lack of external guarantors would mean that implementation would rely on internal Afghan commitment to making the agreement work and the regional powers' willingness to at least avoid destructive interference.

Spoilers on All Sides Will Need to Be Contained

Means will be needed for containing spoilers internal to Afghanistan: those individuals or groups on any side of the conflict that oppose the terms and wish to see the settlement fail. The main way to mitigate this risk in the negotiation phase will be to achieve the greatest extent of consensus on and genuine commitment to the settlement as possible. In the implementation phase, each side will need to exercise responsibility for managing the potential spoilers within its ranks. Similarly, each side will need to police those among its ranks who might attempt reprisals against their former foes.

Transitional Government and Security Arrangements Could Become Stuck

The shift from transitional to permanent government and security arrangements could stall. If, for instance, the constitutional reform process becomes deadlocked, or if controversial aspects of the political settlement are left ambiguous and resolution is deferred to the implementation phase, then the transitional governance arrangements could become stuck in place, leaving Afghanistan in a politically and institutionally weakened condition. Furthermore, because of the difficulty of reconstituting the security forces, the transitional security arrangements could remain in effect for a protracted period of time, which could harden the temporary territorial division of areas of security responsibility.

Afghanistan Will Remain Vulnerable to the Effects of Contestation Between External Actors

Building durable peace in Afghanistan will require support from—or at least noninterference on the part of—a group of countries that are not naturally close collaborators and are, in some cases, outright competitors. Aside from the United States, which will need to lead Western support for implementation of a settlement, this group includes Pakistan, Iran, China, Russia, and India. Each of these countries has long had one or more favored clients within Afghanistan. When the terms of any settlement begin to emerge, these states will likely evaluate those terms relative to their own interests in advancing the positions of their Afghan clients. In addition, it is unlikely that any settlement could enjoy the wholehearted support of both Pakistan and India, which have treated Afghanistan as a theater for competition. Growing tensions between the United States and Iran could affect Iran's willingness to support a negotiated outcome influenced greatly by the United States. But Iran will need to weigh its disinterest in falling in step with U.S. policy in Afghanistan against its interest in the stability of its neighbor.

Policy Recommendations

Beyond the specific recommendations infused in our peace agreement, including alternative options, we offer several broader policy recommendations for the internal and external negotiating parties.

Aim for a Substantive Peace Agreement, Not a Process Roadmap

As of late 2019, it was uncertain whether negotiators would aim to conclude a comprehensive settlement that solves the problem of power-sharing in political and security domains or aim for a more minimalist, process-oriented agreement, like the 2001 Bonn Agreement, that lays out a roadmap for eventually solving that problem. Although negotiating a substantive settlement would obviously be more difficult and time-consuming than negotiating a process roadmap, it is, in the end, the lower-risk approach. Filling in the more difficult details down the road will be harder, not easier, once international attention turns away as a result of an agreement being reached, and once the United States' hard leverage associated with its military presence dissipates. Our recommendation, therefore, is to avoid being under-ambitious. The more partial an agreement is, the more fragile it is likely to be.

Link the Internal and External Aspects of a Settlement

The less intertwined the external and internal elements of an agreement are, the more fragile it is likely to be. External leverage—specifically, U.S. backing for the Afghan security forces and government and U.S. capability to satisfy, or not, the Taliban demand for foreign military withdrawal—is a powerful variable in determining whether a political settlement can be reached and implemented. Concluding a separate peace between the United States and the Taliban would pose the risk of that bilateral accord being carried out regardless of the status of an

Afghan peace process. If the expenditure of external leverage (already a wasting asset in recent years) is not tied to implementation of commitments among Afghans but instead is exhausted early on, then implementation will be less certain.

As the work presented in this report proceeded, U.S. policy shifted toward accepting the Taliban's preferred bifurcation of negotiations into a U.S.-Taliban track focused on the issue of foreign troop withdrawal and a possible subsequent intra-Afghan track. Thus, the likelihood of separate agreements has increased. We have not, however, modified our recommended tying together of the external and internal elements, which is reflected in the structure of our agreement.

Draft Preferred Outcomes Early in the Negotiating Process

Each negotiating party should develop its own preferred version of an agreement early in the peace process. The results of such an exercise can provide each party with directional guidance as it negotiates toward its goals. The process of developing a preferred agreement can enable a party to develop internal consensus, work out the details of negotiating positions and offers, and imagine compromises.

Provide Expert Assistance for Shaping Negotiating Positions and Compromises

The Afghan parties are currently only at the starting gates of substantive preparation for talks. The international sponsors and supporters of a peace process who have a stake in the outcome should ensure that any help the parties might accept in transforming their goals into practical proposals and in designing compromises will be forthcoming. If and when talks among Afghan parties are set, the organizers will need to ensure that a neutral process manager prepares draft agreement text based on the parties' proposals and perhaps also on the manager's own suggested compromises.

Anticipate the Need for Donors to Help Fund Implementation

Foreign donors to Afghanistan should not be penny-wise and pound-foolish. Even though foreign financial support for a postagreement Afghanistan cannot guarantee successful implementation, not providing adequate support to help enable a new government structure to function and the reconfiguration of security forces to be effectuated would virtually guarantee implementation failure. Moreover, Afghanistan's political landscape consists of competing patronage networks, all of which are dependent on either foreign assistance or criminal activity. Such dependence is not a new phenomenon and history suggests that the withdrawal of foreign aid would exacerbate the competition for resources. This competition would pose one of the greatest risks of return to violent conflict.

Abbreviations

APAPPS	Afghanistan-Pakistan Action Plan for Peace and Solidarity
AREU	Afghanistan Research and Evaluation Unit
CNDP	National Congress for the Defense of the People [Congrès National pour la Défense du Peuple]
ICRC	International Committee of the Red Cross
IFOR	Implementation Force (NATO-led, in Bosnia)
ISIS-Khorasan	Islamic State in Iraq and Syria–Khorasan Province
NATO	North Atlantic Treaty Organization
ONUSAL	United Nations Observer Mission in El Salvador
PAM	Peace Accords Matrix
PA-X	Peace Agreements Database
RUF	Revolutionary United Front
UNHCR	United Nations High Commissioner for Refugees
UNITA	National Union for the Total Independence of Angola
UNTAC	United Nations Transitional Authority in Cambodia

CHAPTER ONE

Introduction

Throughout the conflict that followed the 2001 U.S. military intervention in Afghanistan, all three primary belligerents—the United States, the Afghan government, and the Taliban—have intermittently tried to catalyze a peace process. A panoply of nongovernmental organizations, "track two" dialogue organizers, and diplomats from Afghanistan's neighboring states, Europe, and the Gulf region have tried to encourage and facilitate negotiations among the conflict parties. Ending the war through political reconciliation has been a stated goal of Afghanistan's official policy at least since the Afghan government established a High Peace Council in 2010. In early 2011, after two years of laying groundwork, the United States unveiled what appeared to be its own unambiguous policy in favor of peace negotiations: then Secretary of State Hillary Clinton announced that the United States was "launching a diplomatic surge to move this conflict toward a political outcome."[1] In 2013, the Taliban established a political office in Doha, Qatar, explicitly for purposes of negotiating, after sending multiple peace feelers throughout prior years.[2] The conflict parties have

[1] U.S. Department of State, "Remarks at the Launch of the Asia Society's Series of Richard C. Holbrooke Memorial Address," February 18, 2011. This speech also publicly articulated the United States' long-standing end-state conditions: "Over the past two years, we have laid out our unambiguous red lines for reconciliation with the insurgents: They must renounce violence; they must abandon their alliance with al-Qaida; and they must abide by the constitution of Afghanistan. Those are necessary outcomes of any negotiation."

[2] This office formally closed within days of its opening, but the Taliban representatives remained and conducted informal talks with various government representatives and others.

engaged in many direct and indirect informal contacts as well as more formal interactions, including between the United States and the Taliban beginning in late 2010.[3]

As of late 2019, none of these efforts had yet succeeded in launching a sustained, comprehensive negotiating process involving all of the conflict parties, much less delivered peace.[4] In the first half of 2019, as preparation of this report was in the final stage, direct, overt talks between the United States and the Taliban began to gain traction and reportedly were moving beyond preliminaries to core issues, focused particularly on the questions of when and under what conditions the U.S. military would withdraw from Afghanistan. This development was spurred by an energized U.S. diplomatic initiative motivated by the Trump administration's expressed interest in reducing and possibly ending altogether the U.S. military engagement in Afghanistan. In early September 2019, U.S.-Taliban talks nearly produced a preliminary, bilateral agreement but then veered off course.[5] At the time of this report's publication, it was uncertain whether the talks would resume and pave the way to a sustained peace process among Afghans, potentially culminating in a final agreement among the conflict parties. The possibility remained that the United States would abandon negotiations and withdraw most or all of its military forces from Afghanistan nonetheless.[6] If that occurred, the prospects for an Afghan peace process would become exceedingly dim.

---

3 Marc Grossman, "Talking to the Taliban 2011–2012: A Reflection," *Prism*, Vol. 4, No. 4, 2014. This article describes much of the first phase of U.S. direct talks with the Taliban during 2011 and ending in March 2012. The initial U.S. contact with the Taliban was in November 2010, when Richard Holbrooke was the U.S. Special Representative for Afghanistan and Pakistan (Grossman succeeded him after Holbrooke's death).

4 In 2018, the war in Afghanistan was the world's deadliest conflict. Roudabeh Kishi and Melissa Pavlik, *ACLED 2018: The Year in Review*, Madison, Wisc.: Armed Conflict Location and Event Data Project, January 11, 2019.

5 See Laurel Miller and Graeme Smith, "Behind Trump's Taliban Debacle," International Crisis Group, September 10, 2019.

6 For a discussion of the risks of a U.S. military withdrawal from Afghanistan without a peace agreement, see James Dobbins, Jason H. Campbell, Sean Mann, and Laurel E. Miller, *Consequences of a Precipitous Withdrawal from Afghanistan*, Santa Monica, Calif.: RAND Corporation, PE-326-RC, 2019.

The progress that had occurred in U.S.-Taliban talks during 2019 was attributable to a change in U.S. policy. Washington set aside its long-standing insistence that any substantive negotiations had to include the Afghan government's participation and acceded to the Taliban's demand that an understanding on withdrawal of foreign forces be reached in talks solely with the United States prior to commencement of peace talks among Afghans. This bifurcation and sequencing of negotiations suggested that any substantive deals reached might be split as well, into a bilateral U.S.-Taliban agreement and an intra-Afghan agreement.

A full exploration of the many reasons why a peace process failed to launch over years of halting attempts is beyond the scope of this report. One factor is that commitment of the parties to setting a process in motion has been inconsistent, and occasional spikes in each party's desire to negotiate did not coincide. The impulse of each side to seek a stronger position on the battlefield prior to negotiating—or, by some on each side, to continue aiming to win the war—often swamped interest in talks, even well past the time when many officials and observers acknowledged the implausibility of military victory by any side.[7]

A further reason is that the current conflict is in many respects a phase of a four-decade-long war in Afghanistan, marked by shifting alliances, reconfigured entities engaged in the fight, and persistently unresolved grievances. Viewed from this wider perspective, the conflict has been purportedly settled multiple times in that period, the earliest being the Soviet withdrawal and the 1988 Geneva Accords and latest being the U.S.-led overthrow of the Taliban and the process the 2001

[7] For the United States in this regard, see, e.g., White House, "Remarks by President Trump on the Strategy in Afghanistan and South Asia," August 21, 2017, in which Trump stated, "Someday, *after an effective military effort*, perhaps it will be possible to have a political settlement that includes elements of the Taliban in Afghanistan, but nobody knows if or when that will ever happen" (emphasis added). The Trump administration's accelerated effort to negotiate terms for a U.S. withdrawal commenced just over a year later with the appointment of a new Special Representative for Afghanistan Reconciliation, Zalmay Khalilzad.

Bonn Agreement set in motion.[8] The deep-rooted conflict dynamics in this larger picture confound consideration of how to shape an effective peace process.

With respect to the post-2001 conflict phase, another factor has been the lack of a shared perception of who precisely the conflict actors are and what their roles should be in resolving the conflict. The Afghan government has at times asserted that Pakistan is the true aggressor with which Afghanistan needs to make peace.[9] The Taliban have portrayed the Afghan government as a puppet regime and have prioritized dealing instead with the United States, which the Taliban regard as the more authoritative power. At the same time, the persistence of Pakistan's policy of allowing safe haven for the Taliban and the U.S. policy of propping up the Afghan government and its security forces have distorted the calculations the Afghan parties might otherwise have made about their interests in and need for reaching accommodations with each other.

These and many other complications have muddied analysis of the realistic prospects for peacemaking in Afghanistan. An elemental question is whether the conflict parties are genuinely willing to make the compromises necessary to achieve a negotiated peace and accept the risks to their political and security interests inherent in compromises. A reliable answer to this question can only be found through a negotiating process that tests the possibility of "yes." A question that notionally can be answered analytically is whether the interests and goals of the main conflict actors sufficiently overlap or can be brought into sufficient alignment to form the basis for an agreement ending the war.

In principle, the parties' political visions of an Afghanistan at peace and proposals for how to realize those visions can be examined to identify areas of actual or potential coincidence. In reality, how-

---

8 For a detailed treatment of this history, see Peter Tomsen, *The Wars of Afghanistan: Messianic Terrorism, Tribal Conflicts, and the Failures of Great Powers*, New York: Public Affairs, 2011.

9 See, e.g., Eltaf Najafizada and Chris Kay, "Ghani Says Afghanistan Hit by 'Undeclared War' from Pakistan," Bloomberg, June 6, 2017.

ever, those visions remain obscure and underdeveloped. A pronounced absence of articulating what a political settlement might look like has marked the discussions among the conflict actors over the years about the possibility of peace talks as well as the public statements of all sides. None of the conflict parties and no analytical observer of peace initiatives in Afghanistan has put forward a comprehensive set of ideas regarding desired or plausible outcomes of a peace process.[10]

The lack of detailed analysis and policy spelling out the issues likely to arise in a peace process and potential substantive solutions has been one of the obstacles to moving a process forward. Overcoming resistance on the part of conflict actors who have long been invested in prosecution of the war, or who fear what compromise with the enemy might bring, is made more difficult by the absence of a plausible depiction of a political settlement. The purpose of the work presented in this report is to paint such a picture for policymakers on all sides of the conflict and for others interested in encouraging negotiations.

Why We Present Our Analysis in Peace Agreement Form

To show concretely what the outcome of negotiations could look like, we have chosen to write a peace agreement rather than only write about one. That is, instead of offering a narrative analysis of issues and options, we have translated our research and analysis into the format of a comprehensive peace accord. Our intention is not to present this document as a model agreement in a normative sense; we do not claim that the draft agreement represents a set of international best practices (a claim that would be difficult to sustain in any event, given the tre-

---

[10] Perhaps the best, most wide-ranging contribution to analysis of the potential *substance* of a negotiated settlement is Anna Larson and Alexander Ramsbotham, eds., "Incremental Peace in Afghanistan," *Accord*, No. 27, June 2018 (entire issue). Vastly more has been written about how a *process* for negotiating peace might be organized; one of the best contributions along these lines is James Shinn and James Dobbins, *Afghan Peace Talks: A Primer*, Santa Monica, Calif.: RAND Corporation, MG-1131-RC, 2011. This report provides process recommendations that are still largely relevant eight years after publication and also catalogs the likely objectives of actors in a peace process, including those internal to Afghanistan and Afghanistan's neighboring and near-neighboring states.

mendous global diversity of peace agreements). Nor does the document represent the authors' preferences or analytical judgments about the most desirable terms for an Afghan peace agreement. Rather, our intent is to lay out conceivable compromises on the likely most important issues, in a form that would stand some chance of actually being implemented. The result, therefore, does not reflect any one conflict party's preferred set of solutions. We hope that this approach will help the parties envision a final peace agreement and develop realistic negotiating positions toward that end.[11]

Readers will see that the draft agreement includes, in the footnotes, alternative options for many of the proffered terms, particularly on issues likely to be most contentious. This approach reflects the reality that there is not one distinct most-plausible solution for many issues. It also enables the document to better serve as a source of ideas for negotiators and others than if we had limited ourselves to a single proposal for each issue. Even with the presentation of multiple options, we found that the process of working within the structure and language of peace agreement text—as negotiators will need to do—disciplined our analysis and compelled us to reach specific conclusions to a greater extent than would have a narrative approach.

---

11 One of the reviewers of this report commented that, rather than intra-Afghan talks producing a signed peace accord as the final outcome of a peace process, a better approach would be for the outcome of such talks to be presented to a *Loya Jirga* [grand assembly] of Afghans representing a broad range of constituencies, who would deliberate upon and approve—or not, or modify—the outcome of negotiations. In such an assembly, Afghans would participate as individual citizens, not as political representatives, and they would make decisions according to rules established by the assembly itself. It was suggested that one benefit of such an approach would be avoidance of institutionalizing the Taliban as a permanent part of the Afghan state.

Although this is an alternative approach worth considering and would at least theoretically produce a result that enjoys greater popular legitimacy, our assessment is that the uncertainty it would produce in an already fragile situation would make both the negotiations and implementation more difficult. For negotiations, the parties could not be sure that the results would bind anyone. For implementation, there would be many questions as to who would exercise the most influence over constituting the Loya Jirga, and the incentives to skew (or corrupt) the composition would be great. Moreover, the Taliban probably would reject such an approach because of the benefit to them that it avoids. At least to some extent, the legitimacy deficit of the approach we suggest could be addressed through the constitution-making process that would follow from the conclusion of a peace agreement.

How We Developed the Peace Agreement

We grounded our development of the peace agreement in research involving three main types of sources. The first was published material describing the interests and probable goals of the conflict parties related to a potential peace process, including both secondary literature and public remarks of official representatives of the parties. The available secondary literature assessing what the conflict parties would probably want to achieve through a peace process is limited.[12] The second type of source was past peace agreements, for Afghanistan and for many other countries around the world. Our comparative research on peace agreements is presented in Chapter Four. The third was in-person confidential consultations, primarily during the second half of 2018, with approximately 85 individuals associated in their current or former positions with all sides of the conflict and with states neighboring Afghanistan.[13] Afghans represented by far the largest segment of these consultations. Some of these consultations were with academic and think tank experts on Afghanistan and peace processes.

In our comparative research, rather than looking for past peace agreements that more or less in totality could serve as models for Afghanistan, we instead took a cross-cutting, thematic approach. After identifying the issues likely to arise in an Afghan peace process, we searched past peace agreements for examples of how similar issues have been addressed. We also used our review of peace agreements to identify additional issues to address in our text and to find useful examples of agreement structuring. In other words, we treated the past agreements as sources of ideas and inspiration for substance, format, and

---

[12] Examples include Larson and Ramsbotham, 2018; Borhan Osman and Anand Gopal, *Taliban Views on a Future State*, New York: New York University Center on International Cooperation, July 2016; Sean Kane, "Talking with the Taliban: Should the Afghan Constitution Be a Point of Negotiation?" Washington, D.C.: U.S. Institute of Peace, January 2015; Moeed Yusuf, Huma Yusuf, and Salman Zaidi, "Pakistan, the United States and the End Game in Afghanistan: Perceptions of Pakistan's Foreign Policy Elite," Washington, D.C.: U.S. Institute of Peace, July 25, 2011.

[13] This research was reviewed and considered exempt by RAND's Human Subjects Protection Committee (ID 2018-0565). The utmost care was taken to protect the confidentiality of the individuals consulted.

specific wording rather than looking for ready-made blueprints. Chapter Four explains this method and the specific sources in more detail, and the bibliography lists agreements we found particularly useful. We judged that trying to identify a limited number of entire agreements that could serve as models would be a less useful approach, partly because it would constrain the scope of our research but also because peace agreements—being negotiated documents—are highly context-specific. Identifying agreements to serve as models would require analogizing the Afghan context to those of the models' contexts; when we considered a few candidates, the differences in context were evidently greater than the similarities.

We used the consultations both to elicit, through open-ended discussion, ideas for how to resolve specific issues and to seek feedback on ideas as we developed them. For the latter purpose, we shared versions of the agreement with many of those consulted and invited written reactions, which some provided. Because we used the consultations to try out ideas, we modified the text of the agreement through multiple iterations as the work was underway. The final iteration was shared with many individuals who had been consulted in person, as well as others who indicated their willingness to respond with reactions. We used this process to continue testing the plausibility of our text while preparing this report and to share the ideas being developed with officials and others contemporaneously engaged in pursuing a peace process. We do not purport, however, that the final agreement is a mediated or negotiated document; it is solely the product of the authors' independent work.

The greatest challenge in our research was that both the private consultations and publicly available written material revealed that very little work has been done in official policy or nonofficial analyses to develop specific positions or ideas regarding desired outcomes of a peace process. During consultations, it was apparent that none of the conflict parties had developed detailed positions on some of the most consequential issues. It was also apparent that, on each side of the conflict, little progress had been made in building political and bureaucratic consensus around specific objectives for a peace process. Eliciting in-depth feedback on our ideas was therefore difficult with many interlocutors given the nascent stage of policy development.

Although we undertook the research and analysis underlying the agreement in an objective fashion, drafting the text of the agreement necessarily required application of subjective judgments regarding particular provisions' probable acceptability to the parties, feasibility for implementation, and utility in promoting durable peace. Our drafting work thus roughly approximated the role a neutral mediator or facilitator often plays in developing text during a peace negotiation.

Using the first two categories of research inputs, we drafted the first iteration of a complete agreement prior to commencing consultations, and then revised and refined the text as we proceeded. The text is not a mechanistically produced blend of the parties' interests and likely negotiating positions. We assessed that different parties' interests on different issues would not be equally weighted in the real world of negotiating compromises. We also took the view that envisioning outcomes of a peace process required not only identifying maximal demands and minimally acceptable solutions but also trying to anticipate how the parties' positions might evolve over the course of negotiations as their separate demands collide. Imagining how positions might change as a result of both contestation and learning in a peace process was one of the most challenging aspects of our work.

Structure of This Report

Chapter Two identifies the most important issues that would need to be addressed in a peace agreement for Afghanistan, the regional dimensions of an Afghan peace process, how detailed and comprehensive a peace agreement for Afghanistan should be, and the limitations of what an agreement can achieve.

Chapter Three comprises the text of our peace agreement, prefaced by a summary to guide the reader. Accompanying the main agreement are a related Afghanistan-Pakistan bilateral agreement and a "declaration" of supporting states.

Chapter Four presents the comparative research that was an important input to the development of our peace agreement text. This material could be of interest especially to other analysts and researchers, in connection not only with Afghanistan issues but also with other potential peace processes where similar substantive problems arise.

In Chapter Five, the report concludes with an assessment of the degree to which the peace agreement text is likely to satisfy the interests of the conflict parties, identification of key implementation risks, and our policy recommendations.

CHAPTER TWO

Core Substantive Issues to Address in a Peace Agreement for Afghanistan

In this chapter, we summarize (1) the goals of the conflict parties relevant to a peace process and (2) the most important issues for negotiation. Our identification of the goals and issues that will need to be addressed in a peace agreement began with the lead author's assessment based on her prior experience dealing with the conflict actors over several years and working within the U.S. government to advance an Afghan peace process.[1] We refined this initial assessment using our consultations with country experts and relevant political and diplomatic actors, as well as the use of secondary literature. As noted in Chapter One, in many of our consultations, we tested specific ideas as we developed them, but some early consultations with experts were more open-ended as we sought to shape the scope of issues we would address. Although we used our thematic comparative research predominantly to find concepts and wording we could use to solve issues, we also reviewed some peace agreements in their entirety for the purpose of checking that we had sufficiently identified issues (and also for agreement structure ideas). For the latter purpose, we focused on peace agreements for conflicts in which external actors played a major role, such as in Bosnia and Cambodia, but we canvassed others as well.

---

[1] From June 2013 to June 2017, the lead author served as deputy and then acting Special Representative for Afghanistan and Pakistan in the U.S. Department of State.

What Do the Parties Want?

As noted in Chapter One, the extent to which the conflict actors have articulated specific objectives for a peace process is remarkably limited. The Afghan government and anti-Taliban political factions associated with the government and in political opposition have not, as of this writing, forged a consensus on a negotiating platform (nor on the composition of a negotiating team). Nevertheless, Afghan government officials and other politically powerful figures have expressed several general goals:

- a comprehensive and permanent ceasefire
- preservation of democratic and rights-based social gains achieved since 2001
- preservation of the existing constitutional system, perhaps with some unspecified amendments of the 2004 Constitution being negotiable
- continued foreign financial support for Afghanistan.

In general terms, the pro-government side has indicated the acceptability of a reintegration model of peacemaking, in which the Taliban would be offered the opportunity to participate in the current system. In other words, this side most probably would like to see as little change as possible, except for a cessation of hostilities.

The Taliban have clearly stated several goals, the first two of which are paramount:

- removal of all foreign forces from Afghan soil
- establishment of an Islamic system of governance and, toward that end, either a new or modified constitution
- release of all Taliban prisoners
- elimination of United Nations and U.S. sanctions imposed on the organization and many of its leaders, including the Haqqani faction
- normalized relations with foreign governments, including the United States, and continued material support for Afghanistan.

What the Taliban mean by an Islamic government and how that would differ from the current structure and authorities of the post-2001 Islamic Republic is not clear. Nor have the Taliban yet explained the scope of differences with the current constitution that they would demand in revising or replacing the document. In 1998, Taliban religious scholars drafted a constitution for the Islamic Emirate regime, but the Taliban Amir, Mullah Omar, apparently shelved it. The draft appears to have reemerged in Taliban circles in 2005, and leaders may have approved it at that time, but we could not confirm that fact or the document's current status. To the extent that it represents current Taliban thinking, it is worth noting that the document differs in many respects from the 2004 Constitution of the Islamic Republic. A fundamental distinction is that the Taliban document, not surprisingly, provides for an Amir al-Mu'minin [Amir of the believers] to be the paramount leader of Afghanistan; the method for his selection is unspecified. The governance structure includes other positions and bodies with duties specified in the document but does not include democratic elections.[2]

Despite its greater policymaking capacity than the other parties, the United States has been equally slow to develop specific objectives for a peace process. One among many reasons for that reluctance is that U.S. goals in Afghanistan in general have never achieved a high degree of coherence and consistency over time. Bureaucratic and political disagreements over whether, when, and how to pursue peace negotiations have been a particular factor. Nevertheless, the United States clearly has a single overriding goal for the outcome of negotiations:

- assurance that Afghanistan does not again become a sanctuary for al Qaeda or any other terrorist groups that might pose a threat to the United States.

Whether the withdrawal of U.S. military forces from Afghanistan should also be considered a goal in and of itself is uncertain; President

2 For additional description of the document, see Mujib Mashal, "What Do the Taliban Want in Afghanistan? A Lost Constitution Offers Clues," *New York Times*, June 28, 2019.

Donald Trump has repeatedly stated his desire for the military mission to end. Less clear is what conditions, if any, he will attach to withdrawal beyond counterterrorism-related assurances.

A difficulty for the United States is determining what subsidiary objectives must be met to achieve its overriding goal, given that bare rhetorical assurances from the Taliban are not likely to be deemed sufficient, and reliance on the capabilities of the Afghan government security forces might not be considered sufficient either. Questions the United States will need to answer in its policy deliberations include the following:

- Is maintaining a scaled-down U.S. counterterrorism capability in Afghanistan for an indeterminate period of time a "must-have" or "nice-to-have" element of a negotiated settlement?[3]
- Is the United States prepared to abandon development of and partnering with Afghan security forces if objections to such activities are a redline for the Taliban?
- Should the United States be indifferent to the substance of any understandings reached among the Afghan parties on the nature of Afghanistan's governance arrangements, security force architecture, and protections of women's and minorities' rights?

Issues for the Negotiating Agenda

Undoubtedly, the negotiating parties will raise issues and demands that cannot readily be anticipated in advance. Nevertheless, there are several identifiable issues that, at a minimum, will need to be resolved through negotiation to achieve a comprehensive political settlement. Next, we describe the most important and difficult of these issues, which include the following:

---

3 During 2018, our research indicated that maintaining a residual, indefinite military presence for counterterrorism purposes would be a U.S. requirement for a peace agreement, but by the middle of 2019, this position appeared to have softened as the United States negotiated bilaterally with the Taliban with increasing urgency.

- ceasefire and cessation of hostilities
- foreign military presence
- political power-sharing
- security power-sharing
- constitutional reform
- transitional arrangements
- monitoring and verification
- implementation.

Some additional issues that are covered in our peace agreement in Chapter Three and are likely to be on the negotiating agenda are relatively more straightforward, including, for instance, prisoner releases and sanctions relief.

Ceasefire and Cessation of Hostilities

Reciprocal commitments among the conflict parties to ending hostilities are a definitive requirement for a peace agreement. This issue has many important implications, including whether and how adherence to the commitments will be monitored and verified. The key threshold question is when the commitments would come into effect. At a minimum, the effective date would need to be at the time an agreement is concluded, though it is possible—and desirable—to agree on one or more ceasefires earlier in the process.

Foreign Military Presence

Because of the Taliban's assertion of an absolute requirement that foreign troops withdraw from Afghanistan's territory, a negotiated settlement cannot plausibly avoid this issue. For the United States, this issue is linked to its concerns regarding the potential for transnational terrorist groups to threaten its interests from Afghanistan. In light of the original U.S. motivation for invading Afghanistan, an undertaking to withdraw forces will have to be paired with a Taliban renunciation of links with al Qaeda.

Beyond these basic parameters, key questions for negotiation will include whether the withdrawal is complete (as the Taliban have so far insisted) or whether some elements of foreign forces can remain for counterterrorism (including against the Islamic State branch active in Afghanistan) and/or security force assistance purposes. The trigger for beginning withdrawal, the pace of withdrawal, and whether and how it is conditioned on progress toward implementing other elements of the agreement will also have to be negotiated. During 2019, U.S. views on these issues appeared to be moving closer to the Taliban's preferences for speedier and less-conditioned withdrawal.

Political Power-Sharing

For the internal Afghan dimension of a negotiated settlement, the basic premise is that there must be some form of power-sharing. What form that will take is perhaps the most difficult question for Afghan peacemaking. As noted above, pro-government factions are likely to demand as little change to the existing arrangements as possible and will conceive of power-sharing as the integration of the Taliban into the existing political system. The Taliban have rejected an integration model but have not made clear what alternative they will propose. All sides articulate their goals in terms of general principles of inclusivity, broad representation, and maintaining the unity and integrity of Afghanistan, but without translating those principles into concrete positions thus far.

The Taliban appear to reject forms of power-sharing that would involve division of the political pie by allocating ministerial and other positions, and all Afghan political elites reject power-sharing on the basis of territorial division. Most also reject at least robust forms of decentralization—which could increase the number of political prizes—as a means of achieving power-sharing, even though many experts believe decentralization would fit Afghanistan's reality better than its historically highly centralized formal government structures. Afghan negotiators are likely to seek de facto assured shares of political power while endeavoring not to be seen as doing so. Consequently, crafting modified governance arrangements that provide such assurances and at least nominally have permanent features of achieving inclusivity will be a major challenge.

Security Power-Sharing

An agreement will have to determine the disposition and authorities of state and nonstate armed forces after the cessation of hostilities. Essential questions will include whether and how the state security forces will be reconfigured to include Taliban elements, whether continued foreign security assistance and partnership is contemplated, and how to ensure protection from retribution for former fighters. In a context in which neither Afghan side is defeated, neither is surrendering, and both control substantial territory, applying a standard "DDR" (disarmament, demobilization, and reintegration) formula to the disposition of the nonstate forces seems unrealistic. An additional problem for negotiating the scope of any demobilization is the multiplicity of militias in Afghanistan, some of which are associated with the government.

For the immediate aftermath of an agreement, it is realistic to assume the Taliban will not be prepared to lay down arms and defer to the existing state security forces. Consequently, determining which armed elements will be responsible for security in what areas of the country—at least until power-sharing and restructuring of state security forces comes into effect—will be crucial. Security tasks will include law and order, protection against retribution, counterterrorism against the Islamic State, and potentially actions against individuals or groups looking to spoil the peace agreement. Lack of negotiated clarity on the role and authorities of armed elements on a territorial basis would risk unraveling a ceasefire.

Constitutional Reform

Issues of both constitutional process and substance will need to be negotiated. The threshold question will be whether the existing 2004 Constitution should be amended or replaced entirely. The Taliban have objected to that constitution on principle because of their exclusion from the process of creating it, but they have not clearly demanded that the document be entirely replaced. They have indicated that the substance is only partly objectionable, but they have not said precisely which parts. The Taliban's insistence on establishing Islamic governance in Afghanistan can be expected to shape their positions on constitutional issues—including the structure of government and rights provisions—but any specific positions they might have developed have not been revealed yet. The Afghan government and anti-Taliban political factions can be expected in negotiations to hew closely to the text and amendment procedures in the 2004 Constitution.

Transitional Arrangements

If changes are to be made to Afghan government and security structures under the terms of a peace agreement, then temporary structures and procedures will need to be put in place until the permanent changes are implemented. Transitional arrangements are a typical feature of peace agreements. The temporary arrangements could take effect from the time a comprehensive peace agreement is concluded or earlier, if a series of agreements is concluded in phases.

Political and security transitional arrangements will need to include power-sharing features because it is unlikely that either Afghan side in the conflict will agree to be absorbed into the other in the early stage of agreement implementation. But these features could be different, and probably simplified, as compared with the permanent structures. Crude slicing of the political pie in a fashion that Afghan negotiators probably will find objectionable for the permanent structures might be acceptable for a transitional period.

Monitoring and Verification

All sides will likely seek procedures and mechanisms to assure, as far as possible, the others' fulfillment of commitments. The United States will probably want verification and perhaps means for enforcement of Taliban counterterrorism commitments. The Taliban appear to desire international guarantees of U.S. commitments. And the Afghan government and anti-Taliban factions will be concerned about verification and enforcement of the full range of Taliban commitments.

Establishment of an international peacekeeping or peace enforcement mission for Afghanistan is implausible. Regardless of the views of Afghan negotiators, states that would have appropriate capabilities and sufficient neutrality to contribute to any such mission are unlikely to be interested after nearly two decades of extraordinary financial and military investments in Afghanistan. Negotiators will therefore need to focus on developing as robust a set of monitoring and verification mechanisms as feasible.

Implementation

The two basic implementation issues are (1) how the Afghan parties will arrange their coordination of implementation and means for resolving inevitable disputes and (2) how external actors will support implementation. The second issue implies negotiation and agreement between the Afghan parties on seeking support and, with the external parties, negotiation of the statements of support that will be on offer. In addition to financial assistance and roles in monitoring and verification, external support could include involvement in mediating implementation disputes. The Afghan parties' willingness to invite such mediation could be an indicator of good-faith commitment to comply with the agreement and could help build mutual confidence.

The Regional Dimension of an Afghan Peace Process

An Afghan peace agreement will need to attract the support of regional states if it is to successfully provide a basis for durable peace. Afghanistan's neighbors and near-neighbors have long interfered in its affairs and have stoked conflict within its borders.[4] Many declarations and agreements to abjure such interference have, in important respects,

---

[4] For discussion of this complex problem, see, for example, Barnett R. Rubin, "Everyone Wants a Piece of Afghanistan," *Foreign Policy*, March 11, 2019. Rubin explains the need for regional consensus over the shape of Afghanistan's security architecture and how it will be externally supported if an agreement leading to an American troop withdrawal is not to lead to the collapse of the Afghan government, as happened after the 1988 Geneva Accords related to the Soviet withdrawal. See also Gareth Price, "Afghanistan and Its Neighbours: Forging Regional Engagement," London: Chatham House, May 2015. For a thorough treatment of neighboring and broader regional states' impact on conflict in Afghanistan, see Kristian Berg Harpviken and Shahrbanou Tadjbakhsh, *A Rock Between Hard Places: Afghanistan as an Arena of Regional Insecurity*, New York: Oxford University Press, 2016. For discussion of the likely goals of regional states related to an Afghan peace process, see Shinn and Dobbins, 2011, pp. 39–48 and 52–69.

been routinely violated.[5] Pakistan's role in perpetuating the Afghan conflict by allowing the Taliban safe haven within its territory and Pakistan's perception of Afghanistan as within its legitimate sphere of influence mean that its support for resolution of the conflict will be especially crucial.

Regional governments have been reluctant to express views on what the substantive outcomes of an Afghan peace process should be, generally claiming only to be interested in any result that produces Afghan stability. One aspect of an agreement that will certainly be of interest is the pace and manner of a U.S. and North Atlantic Treaty Organization (NATO) military drawdown. Of the most influential regional states, only India prefers a long-term U.S. military presence in Afghanistan. The others—China, Iran, Pakistan, and Russia—have, over the past two decades, been conflicted about the U.S. military presence. They have wanted the United States not to withdraw from Afghanistan too quickly (thus risking collapse of the state) and not to stay permanently, with military bases in their backyards. These states will likely welcome a U.S. commitment to withdraw completely or almost completely but probably will be concerned if the withdrawal arrangements are not tied to completion of an Afghan political settlement.

The role of regional states in Afghan peace negotiations will largely be behind the scenes and might not be overtly reflected in the substance of a peace agreement. One way in which their role can manifest is through witnessing signature of an agreement (meaning that they would also sign the agreement as witnesses but not as parties to its terms). This common procedure has no legal effect, but it implies that the witnessing states have interests in seeing an agreement imple-

---

[5] One example is Transitional Administration of Afghanistan and Governments of China, the Islamic Republic of Iran, Pakistan, Tajikistan, Turkmenistan, and Uzbekistan, Kabul Declaration on Good-Neighbourly Relations, Kabul, Afghanistan, December 22, 2002; another is Republic of Afghanistan and Islamic Republic of Pakistan, Bilateral Agreement Between the Republic of Afghanistan and the Islamic Republic of Pakistan on the Principles of Mutual Relations, in Particular on Non-Interference and Non-Intervention, Geneva, Switzerland, April 14, 1988b, which was Annex I of the 1988 Geneva Accords.

mented. For Afghanistan, this procedure could signify that the witnessing states believe they have stakes in the settlement of the conflict, that they were engaged in the diplomacy undergirding the agreement, and that the agreement enjoys their approval. Because of the significance of the regional dimension of the Afghan conflict, the Afghan parties and external actors probably would also consider packaging a peace agreement with accompanying agreements or declarations relating to foreign support for its implementation.

How Detailed and Comprehensive Should the Peace Agreement Be?

The question of how detailed the agreement text should be elicited divergent reactions during consultations. In contrast to the approach we adopted, some argued for less prescriptiveness and more flexibility for Afghans to deliberate and agree on specifics of governance and security arrangements *after* a more minimalist peace agreement is concluded. (It should be noted, however, that the agreement text presented in Chapter Three is on the lower end of the range of length and detail of the peace agreements we reviewed in our comparative research.)

In actual Afghan peace negotiations, and thus in the text we drafted, a balance has to be struck between addressing enough issues in sufficient detail that the resultant agreement adequately speaks to the aims and interests of all parties and not overloading the circuits with more issues than can successfully be brought to resolution in a reasonable amount of time. One example of an issue that, although important, we have left out of our text is the problem of vast illicit economic activity linked to perpetuation of conflict in Afghanistan. We assessed that an Afghan peace agreement is unlikely to solve this complex problem to any meaningful extent.

Several considerations guided our determination of how ambitious the scope of the agreement text should be. First, the pressure of a peace negotiation and the intense international attention focused on it creates a window of opportunity for forging compromises that is lost once an agreement is concluded. When the pressure dissipates and the spotlight shifts away, incentives to compromise diminish. Second, some have suggested that the ambiguity of a less detailed text could be helpful in overcoming obstacles in negotiations; however, especially in such a low-trust environment as Afghanistan, ambiguity can simply cloak obstacles temporarily. A relatively more ambiguous agreement might fall apart once the differences that were not actually overcome reemerge. Third, an agreement that kicks too many difficult issues down the road (for instance, by referring them to implementation commissions or other postagreement procedures) will introduce a degree of uncertainty about the commitments undertaken that is likely to make carrying out the peace agreement and verifying adherence to its terms problematic.[6] In other words, a simpler text might be easier to negotiate but would be more difficult to implement, with deferred issues likely remaining unresolved indefinitely, particularly when foreign troops, money, and attention diminish.

Our conceptual starting point for drafting the agreement text was a do-over of the late-2001 Bonn Agreement that set out a process and basic principles for establishing governance arrangements in the aftermath of the U.S. ouster of the Taliban regime.[7] This less-than-eight-page agreement established an Interim Authority for governing Afghanistan and a process roadmap for creating a transitional authority and a new constitution under which elections for permanent government structures would be held within several years. It set in motion

---

6 Two recent examples of such agreements in Afghanistan are the political agreement establishing the National Unity Government (National Unity Government of the Islamic Republic of Afghanistan et al., Afghanistan and International Community: Commitments to Reforms and Renewed Partnership, London, December 4, 2014) and the reconciliation agreement between the Government of the Islamic Republic of Afghanistan and Hizb-e Islami of Afghanistan (Government of the Islamic Republic of Afghanistan and Hizb-e Islami of Afghanistan, Agreement, Kabul, Afghanistan, September 22, 2016). Both of these agreements referred the most contentious issues to subsequent elaboration, and both have been only partially implemented.

7 Agreement on Provisional Arrangements in Afghanistan Pending the Re-Establishment of Permanent Government Institutions ("Bonn Agreement"), Bonn, Germany, December 5, 2001.

the reconstitution of the Afghan state on the basis of consensus reached among leaders of Afghan political factions who participated in United Nations–organized talks. Those talks excluded the Taliban, though the Bonn Agreement anticipated, albeit vaguely, the need to ensure inclusion of elements associated with the Taliban by noting that "groups that have not been adequately represented at the UN talks" would need to be represented in governance arrangements. That exclusion was based on the misconception that the Taliban had been definitively defeated. Redoing the Bonn Agreement would mean reconstituting the Afghan state once again, this time with the Taliban's participation.

In our consultations, some suggested that a forthcoming peace agreement could be nearly as simple and roadmap-like as the Bonn Agreement. Using the scoping considerations outlined above, we rejected this approach in favor of a more substantively detailed document addressing a wider range of issues. An additional reason was that the context now is vastly changed from the implementation period for the Bonn Agreement. Bonn was, after all, a gathering of factions united in their opposition to the Taliban and in dependence on the United States for their accession to power. Moreover, that earlier period saw rising international engagement in Afghanistan, including financial and security guarantees bolstering implementation; the current context is one of declining international interest in and support for Afghanistan. International actors, including the United Nations, were deeply involved in facilitating the establishment of a post-Bonn political order and mediating implementation disputes among Afghan factions to an extent that is unlikely nearly two decades later. In the current context, opting for a relatively more elaborate peace agreement by no means assures successful implementation, but it would at least mitigate the potential for disputes over missing details to collapse the deal. A final reason is that the vacuum of state authority in late 2001 justified the simplicity of the Bonn Agreement, whereas understandings now will be needed regarding what to do with existing state structures.

Regardless of the choice peace negotiators make regarding the complexity of an agreement, the text offered in Chapter Three can serve as a resource for identifying issues and options. It can also be used for comparison with the actual results of a peace process to help evaluate issues that have been addressed and identify issues that have been punted. Although we conclude that a more comprehensive agreement should be preferred to a more limited one, our agreement is illustrative, not prescriptive; we did not craft the agreement as an all-or-nothing text. Moreover, an Afghan peace process might, like many others around the world, proceed in stages, with intermediate agreements reached along the way. Under that approach, the agreements could draw from pieces of our text.

Limitations of a Peace Agreement

The problem of establishing durable peace in Afghanistan is larger than the solution offered by any peace agreement, no matter how comprehensively it responds to the grievances and power struggles driving conflict. After more than four decades of violence, of which the post-2001 conflict is the latest phase, a negotiated political settlement that focuses on the latest configuration of conflict actors will be a necessary but insufficient salve.

Although any peace agreement in and of itself is a limited vehicle for conflict resolution, an agreement and the process of compromise and consensus-building that produces it can set a foundation for peace. Ultimately, the will of the parties to make an agreement stick and to resolve the inevitable disputes over implementation that will arise will determine whether the foundation holds or crumbles.

Building on that foundation will require developing a political system that keeps competition in the nonviolent political realm. Many conditions have changed in Afghanistan over the last two decades, but the basic structural conundrum of the Afghan state has not: Afghan political elites predominantly insist on a highly centralized system, but a winner-take-all political apparatus, combined with a deeply entrenched patronage-based political culture and with ethnic and tribal identity politics, has produced persistent internal conflict and left Afghanistan vulnerable to external interference.[8] The agreement text offered in this report points modestly in the direction of some solutions, but actually resolving this conundrum will be a much greater and long-term endeavor.

---

8 On Afghanistan's lack of and need for effective opposition politics, see Thomas Barfield, "Afghanistan's Political History: Prospects for Peaceful Opposition," *Accord*, No. 27, June 2018.

CHAPTER THREE

A Comprehensive Peace Agreement

Summary of Key Provisions

The text of our peace agreement in this chapter is intended to show, as realistically as possible, what a final comprehensive peace agreement for Afghanistan could look like at the end of a negotiating process among the internal and external parties to the conflict.

Portions of the text could potentially be used in separate agreements in a phased manner, if advantageous for achieving negotiating progress. However, the most important issues, particularly those identified below as part of the "core bargain," might be seen by one or more parties as too interdependent to separate into phased agreements.

The following summary provides a guide to the agreement text. The summary is not part of the agreement text. Importantly, footnotes in our peace agreement include some alternatives to the ideas summarized here.

The **structure** comprises

- an Agreement on a Comprehensive Settlement, with Parts I and III including commitments by four parties (Afghan government, Taliban, United States, and North Atlantic Treaty Organization [NATO]) and Part II including commitments of two parties (Taliban and Afghan government)
- an agreement between Afghanistan and Pakistan that would be signed simultaneously with the main Comprehensive Settlement
- a Declaration by supporting states that also would be signed simultaneously with the main Comprehensive Settlement.

Negotiators might want to include, as an additional document, a side agreement among the important pro-government Afghan political parties and factions stating that the Afghan government's signature on the agreement represents the assent of all these groups. Drafting such a side agreement early in the process might help defuse persistent disputes over what would constitute a sufficiently representative negotiating team on the anti-Taliban side.

The **main elements** of the Agreement on a Comprehensive Settlement are the following:

- A **core bargain** involving both the internal and external parties that includes
  - a comprehensive ceasefire and cessation of hostilities
  - a complete renunciation by the Taliban of links with international terrorist groups
  - a complete, phased ending of the current U.S./NATO military mission over an 18-month (but extendable) transitional time period, based on completion of agreement implementation milestones
  - an invitation by the Afghan parties to the international community to form a small, limited "Afghanistan Support Team" focused exclusively on counterterrorism action and assistance, especially against the Islamic State in Iraq and Syria–Khorasan Province, coupled with a request for a named country (determined during negotiations) to organize the team
  - the expressed intention of the United States to continue providing civilian assistance and to solicit contributions from other donors.
- New **political arrangements** within Afghanistan that include
  - inclusivity and broad-based representation as the fundamental guiding principles
  - a process for the adoption of a new constitution within 12 months, with some elements and principles for the new constitution included in the agreement text
  - the 2004 Constitution remaining in effect until adoption of a new constitution, except where inconsistent with the agree-

ment (the process specified in the agreement for adopting a new constitution would be followed instead of the amendment procedures in the 2004 Constitution)
  - a presidential system, with somewhat reduced powers for the president and increased balancing of presidential power compared with the current system
  - a modest degree of devolution of authority to the provincial level of government to promote broad distribution of power among demographic and political groups in areas where they are concentrated and to recalibrate the center-regions relationship (not a shift to federalism, but a shift toward more opportunities for a greater number of political and demographic groups to exercise a share of governmental power)
  - flexibility for governance arrangements at the district level, to create space for localized solutions
  - the establishment of a High Council of Islamic Scholars with roles in evaluating the consistency of legislation with Islamic tenets and principles and in advising the government.
- Establishment of a **Transitional Government** for the 18-month transition period, including a Transitional Executive with a negotiated by-name list of a Chairman, several Vice Chairmen, and members (rotating chairmanship is suggested as an inferior alternative in case the parties cannot agree on a single individual to serve as Chairman).
- **Security arrangements** that include
  - reconstitution of the armed forces to make leadership more inclusive and broadly representative of the population and to provide equitable opportunity for inclusion among the rank and file
  - a single national army, air force, border police, and intelligence service
  - devolution of policing responsibility to the provincial level
  - prohibition of armed groups not explicitly authorized by the state, once reconstitution is completed
  - disarmament only of heavy weapons.

- **Transitional security** arrangements until reconstitution that include
  - forces of each side responsible for security and public order in areas over which they exercise control, in accordance with a negotiated map of areas of responsibility
  - the establishment of a Joint Military Commission with duties including coordinating across areas of responsibility and establishing a joint command structure.
- Broad **amnesty**, consistent with Afghan precedent, balanced with creating a process for promoting **reconciliation**.
- Release of all conflict-related **prisoners/detainees**, based on a negotiated list of persons to be released.
- Request for international assistance with the **return of refugees** and displaced persons.
- Establishment of a process for addressing **land and property** disputes.
- Request for establishment of a **Monitoring and Verification Team** under the "good offices" of the United Nations Secretary-General.
- Removal of all remaining **sanctions** imposed on members of the Taliban in connection with their membership in or activities related to the Taliban, except for any persons who reject the agreement.
- Establishment of a **Joint Implementation Commission** composed of the parties to the agreement, responsible for resolving any disputes over interpretation of the agreement. (If a neutral facilitating or mediating body or state becomes involved in the negotiating process, or if circumstances change to make a peacekeeping body or guarantor become plausible, this Commission should include such a neutral actor. Without a neutral actor involved, the risk is higher that the Commission might not function effectively.)

The text does not include a request for a peacekeeping mission to be organized by or a ceasefire guarantor role to be played by a neutral organization or state. This gap raises the risk of implementation failure but reflects the current lack of appetite within the international community for potentially taking on such responsibilities.

The footnotes throughout the peace agreement text explain the meaning and significance of proposed language where that might not otherwise be apparent. They also include alternative options for proposals in the text, and they provide some selective examples of where ideas and inspiration were drawn from other peace agreements. The footnotes should not be considered part of the agreement text.

Peace Agreement Text

Agreement on a Comprehensive Settlement of the Conflict in Afghanistan

The entirety of this Agreement sets forth a comprehensive settlement of the conflict in Afghanistan among the signatories.[1] Part I of this Agreement comprises binding commitments entered into by the Government of the Islamic Republic of Afghanistan, the Islamic Movement of the Afghan Taliban, the United States of America, and the North Atlantic Treaty Organization ("NATO")[2] (hereafter "the four

---

1 An **alternative structural option** would be to conclude two separate agreements (one between the Afghan Parties and one among the four Parties) that include provisions stating that the two agreements are mutually interdependent. One or both Afghan parties might prefer two separate agreements. However, including all commitments of the various parties in one agreement, as suggested here, could underscore more strongly the interdependence of the internal and the international commitments and could reflect more clearly the negotiating principle that "nothing is agreed until everything is agreed." A **second alternative structural option** would be to conclude one agreement only between the United States (possibly with NATO) and the Taliban and a separate agreement among the Afghan parties. As of mid 2019, in a concession to the Taliban, which had long preferred such a bifurcation of any peace negotiations into "external" and "internal" dimensions, the United States moved in the direction of this second alternative. As of this writing, it was unclear, given this approach, whether and how a U.S./NATO drawdown would be tied to an Afghan political settlement.

2 Including NATO as a party to this Agreement is not intended to suggest that NATO should be a full participant in the negotiating process, which, given NATO's cumbersome

Parties"). Part II of this Agreement comprises binding commitments entered into by the Government of the Islamic Republic of Afghanistan and the Islamic Movement of the Afghan Taliban[3] (hereafter "the Afghan Parties"). Part III ("Final Provisions") comprises further binding commitments of the four Parties. Parts I, II, and III of the Agreement are mutually interdependent and together form a single comprehensive Agreement.

The Agreement Between the Islamic Republic of Afghanistan and the Islamic Republic of Pakistan in Connection with the Agreement on a Comprehensive Settlement of the Conflict in Afghanistan and the Declaration of Supporting States in Connection with the Agreement on a Comprehensive Settlement of the Conflict in Afghanistan are related to this Agreement but are separate instruments. The implementation of these separate instruments will support and facilitate implementation of this Agreement.

Part I

Recognizing and honoring the sacrifices on all sides of the conflict,

Acknowledging and respecting the desire for peace among the people of Afghanistan,

---

decisionmaking procedures, would be an unhelpful complication. NATO is included as a signatory to this Agreement because the United States cannot alone commit to withdrawal of non-U.S. NATO forces.

3 Names and other terminology used in the Agreement to refer to the two Afghan parties could be contentious because of their resistance to acknowledging each other's legitimacy. This text proposes use of the internationally recognized name for the government of Afghanistan. The Taliban might prefer "Islamic Emirate of Afghanistan," which is the name they use to refer to themselves but also is the name of their former regime and therefore is likely to be rejected by the other parties because it could imply that the Taliban signatory has governmental status. Although alternatives to the name suggested here could be feasible, opposition to any use of the term "Emirate" is likely to be a redline for the other parties.

Reaffirming the independence, sovereignty, unity, and territorial integrity of Afghanistan,

Desiring to establish a firm foundation for positive and peaceful relations between Afghanistan and the international community, including the United States and the other members of NATO,

Affirming their commitment to promoting enduring peace and stability in Afghanistan,

Respecting the right of all the people of Afghanistan to freely determine their own political future on the basis of full inclusion of all elements of Afghan society and in accordance with the principles of Islam, democracy, pluralism, and social justice,[4] and

Appreciating the good faith and dignity with which all of the Parties negotiated this Agreement,

The four Parties agree to the following:

Article I.1

COMPREHENSIVE CEASEFIRE, CESSATION OF HOSTILITIES, AND RENUNCIATION OF LINKS WITH INTERNATIONAL TERRORISM

A. In the interests of establishing enduring security and stability in Afghanistan and fostering international peace and security, the

---

[4] This preambular sentence is based on part of the preamble to the Agreement on Provisional Arrangements in Afghanistan Pending the Re-Establishment of Permanent Government Institutions (2001 Bonn Agreement), with the addition of "all" the people and "on the basis of full inclusion of all elements of Afghan society." The other preambular sentences are intended to reflect the essential interests of each of the four Parties and the probable goals of a peace process. An **alternative** to "principles" of Islam could be "provisions and beliefs," as in the 2004 Constitution.

four Parties commit to an immediate, mutual, and comprehensive ceasefire and cessation of hostilities, effective upon signature of this Agreement.

B. The Islamic Movement of the Afghan Taliban renounces unequivocally and permanently any form of links with, including providing any form of support to or receiving any form of support from, any terrorist groups, including al Qaeda and any of its branches or related groups.

C. The Afghan Parties shall prevent any use of the territory or airspace of Afghanistan in any manner that threatens the security of any other state. This includes a commitment not to permit Afghan land or air to be used as a launching point or transit space for attacks against any state.

D. The Afghan Parties further commit to ensuring the removal from Afghan territory of unauthorized foreign fighters and fulfilling Afghanistan's obligation to ensure that international terrorist groups shall find no safe haven within Afghanistan. The Afghan Parties shall cooperate with interested states toward these ends.

Article I.2

WITHDRAWAL OF FOREIGN FORCES

A. Based on the commitments stated in Article I.1, the United States and NATO shall end their current military missions in Afghanistan and withdraw all of their personnel performing military duties and contractor personnel performing and supporting military duties,[5] bringing to a complete close the military intervention that commenced in October 2001.

---

5 This wording is intended to be broad and include any personnel performing or supporting military-type duties regardless of the specific security institution with which these personnel are associated.

B. This withdrawal shall occur in three[6] phases over an expected period of 18 months,[7] in accordance with the following timetable and contingent[8] on achievement of the following milestones:

i. *Phase One* shall be completed within six months of signature of this Agreement. The milestones to be completed within Phase One are
   a. Complete formation of all elements of the Transitional Government, in accordance with Article II.4;
   b. Establishment of the unified transitional command structure for transitional security arrangements, in accordance with Article II.5; and
   c. Formation of the constitution drafting committee, in accordance with Article II.2.

ii. *Phase Two* shall be completed within 12 months of signature of this Agreement. The milestone to be completed within

---

6 An **alternative option** could be four phases, with an initial troop withdrawal tranche beginning upon signature of the Agreement to build confidence that withdrawal will occur. However, dividing up a relatively small number of personnel into four tranches might be infeasible given force protection requirements, which could be of greatest concern early in the transition period.

Another **alternative option** could be to alter the mission or locations of foreign troops upon signature of the Agreement, garrisoning some or all on bases, for example, without yet removing any troops from the country.

7 In peace agreements involving the withdrawal of foreign forces, the timelines vary considerably, from less than one month to about three years in the agreements researched for this proposal.

An **alternative option** could be to provide for a **12-month withdrawal and transition period**. Experts consulted during development of this text strongly viewed 12 months as unrealistically brief in light of likely implementation challenges. Nevertheless, 12 months might be more politically acceptable to both the United States and the Taliban. In addition, a longer transition period might increase the risk of failure of the peace Agreement because power-sharing transitional governments tend to be weak and fractious.

8 "Contingent" is used here to indicate that the timetable would automatically be extended if the milestones are not achieved. An **alternative option** could be to state more explicitly whether the timetable or the milestones take precedence.

Phase Two is completion of the proceedings of an inclusive constitutional assembly[9] and confirmation of the constitution, in accordance with Article II.2.

iii. *Phase Three* shall be completed within 18 months of signature of this Agreement. The milestones to be completed within Phase Three are
   a. Completion of national and provincial elections for positions specified in Article II.3 and in the constitution that shall be confirmed in Phase Two; and
   b. Unification[10] and reconstitution of the army, air force, border police, and intelligence service and decentralization to the provincial level of other policing responsibilities, in accordance with Article II.6.

C. Prior to the end of each phase,[11] the United States and NATO shall notify the Afghan Parties of the numbers of personnel to be withdrawn for that phase and the military facilities and areas to be closed or transferred to Afghan authorities for that phase.[12]

---

9 The generic term "constitutional assembly" is used here to avoid confusion with the term "Constitutional Loya Jirga" used in the 2004 Constitution, a mechanism for which the formation requirements probably cannot be, and need not be, met. Forming a Constitutional Loya Jirga in the way specified in the Constitution requires holding district council elections, which as of early 2019 has not been feasible.

10 The term "unification" is proposed here as a more accurate (and, for the Taliban, likely greatly more acceptable) concept than "reintegration," a term commonly used in other contexts. An alternative term could be "integration."

11 An **alternative option** could be for notification to occur at the start of each phase, but the suggested wording provides more flexibility by allowing notification to occur at any point during the phase. In addition to practical reasons, the notification requirement would be important to ensuring transparency of drawdown plans in order to build confidence among the parties.

12 The numbers of personnel withdrawn in each phase will probably need to differ because of force protection and base security requirements. Depending on how the negotiating process proceeds, the United States and NATO might be able to specify in the Agreement the numbers to be withdrawn in each phase based on planning done prior to the conclusion of the Agreement, but they might also need to retain some flexibility in this regard for practi-

For each phase, withdrawal shall be completed by the end date of the phase, contingent on the milestones for that phase having been implemented.

D. Adherence to the withdrawal timeline is also contingent on continuous implementation of the commitments expressed in Article I.1.[13]

E. The requirement for complete withdrawal of U.S. and NATO military and contractor personnel shall not apply to personnel required for and assigned to security duties for the United States Embassy in Kabul and diplomatic facilities of other NATO member states.[14]

F. If requested by the Transitional Executive established according to Article II.4, during the phased withdrawal process the United States and NATO may provide assistance and training to Afghan authorities with respect to implementing unification of the armed forces, border police, and intelligence service and decentralization of other policing responsibilities. U.S. and NATO personnel subject to the withdrawal requirements in this Article shall undertake no offensive military tasks during the phased withdrawal unless requested to do so by both Afghan

---

cal reasons. Some other peace agreements include more detailed provisions regarding phased withdrawal of foreign forces than proposed here.

13 This provision means that the phasing of the drawdown is, to a limited extent, a means of enforcing the ceasefire and cessation of hostilities because the drawdown could be stopped or slowed if either of the Afghan Parties commits violations. This provision also implies that the Afghan Parties will be responsible for suppressing the actions of potential spoilers over whom they have some control, meaning factions or individuals associated with the Afghan Parties who reject this Agreement and attempt to break the ceasefire.

14 Embassies will likely have military personnel assigned to defense attaché offices, and, if there will be continued U.S. funding provided for Afghan military and police, at least the U.S. Embassy will need to have military personnel assigned to an Office of Security Cooperation to manage the flow of funding. These realities probably need not be stated in the Agreement because such personnel will not be performing security functions.

Parties, except that at all times they shall retain the right of self-defense.[15]

Article I.3

REQUEST OF THE AFGHAN PARTIES FOR COUNTER-TERRORISM SUPPORT[16]

---

15 Although, to a limited extent, the presence of U.S./NATO forces in Afghanistan during the phased withdrawal could deter ceasefire violations by the Afghan Parties, this provision means that U.S./NATO forces would not be directly responsible for enforcing or guaranteeing implementation of the security aspects of the Agreement.

16 A provision such as this, which enables counterterrorism actions and partnership with Afghanistan *during or after* the withdrawal of the current U.S./NATO mission, could be important to attracting U.S. support for the Agreement but probably will be difficult for the Taliban to accept. (The language suggested here is flexible as to whether the Afghanistan Support Team would be created during the phased withdrawal or after it is completed, but that point would need to be clarified during negotiations to prevent conflict over interpretation.)

Whether the Taliban ultimately would accept a provision such as this might depend on the extent of trust that is built during the negotiating process, as well as the extent to which the rest of the Agreement addresses Taliban interests. It might also depend on whether support and encouragement of other countries in the region can be brought to bear. Pakistan likely would support this provision and China probably would (so long as the counterterrorism support is temporary), but Iran and Russia are likely to be more skeptical, perhaps seeing this support as a pretext for a continued U.S. military presence in the region.

To mitigate these difficulties, the language suggested here attempts to draw a clear distinction between a new counterterrorism support mission and the currently existing U.S./NATO mission that would be ended in accordance with this Agreement. This language also attempts to emphasize that an invitation for counterterrorism cooperation would be based on Afghan sovereignty. If the Taliban agreed to such a provision, they might request a gap in time between the end of the current mission and the start of new counterterrorism cooperation, but the United States probably would consider that approach impractical.

Past peace agreements involving withdrawal of foreign forces provide some examples of agreement on a future foreign military role. For instance, the 1962 Algeria-France Évian Accords that ended France's colonial rule and established Algeria's independence included a commitment to lease certain military facilities to France.

An **alternative option** could be to exclude this provision from the Agreement and consider the issue toward the end of the foreign forces' withdrawal period, after some trust might have been built through compliance with the withdrawal terms. However, that approach would leave uncertain the likelihood of reaching later agreement on the issue.

A. The Afghan Parties request temporary and limited assistance from the international community for purposes of supporting Afghanistan in its efforts to maintain security and stability by conducting operations against terrorist organizations in Afghanistan, including the Islamic State in Iraq and Syria–Khorasan Province (ISIS-Khorasan) and al Qaeda. To organize provision of this assistance, the Afghan Parties request [*country name*][17] to establish a new Afghanistan Support Team;[18] [*country name*] shall coordinate with the Afghan Parties in determining which states shall be asked to participate. The Afghanistan Support Team shall not be a continuation of the United States and NATO military missions that shall be ended in accordance with Article I.2. The mandate for the Afghanistan Support Team shall be based on the invitation and consent of the sovereign Afghan state and shall be effective upon signature of this Agreement.

B. All activities of the Afghanistan Support Team shall be conducted with the agreement of the Transitional Government established in accordance with Article II.4 and subsequent governance authorities of Afghanistan; shall respect Afghan sovereignty, customs, and traditions; and shall be fully coordinated

---

[17] The government requested to organize the Afghanistan Support Team would need to accept this responsibility prior to conclusion of the Agreement. An **alternative option** could be to state in this paragraph that the United States and NATO will set up the Afghanistan Support Team and to pre-negotiate that other, especially Muslim-majority, states would play a prominent role in helping to organize and participating in the Team. Implementation of this alternative option could be more practical in some respects because of the counterterrorism and organizational capabilities that the United States and NATO have. However, explicitly referencing agreement to the continued presence of U.S. and NATO forces probably would be unacceptable to the Taliban because of their long-standing position that they are fighting to achieve the removal of such forces from Afghan soil. Nonetheless, the main option included in the text would not exclude participation of U.S. and other NATO personnel if Afghan consent was provided outside the text of the Agreement.

[18] This suggested name ("Afghanistan Support Team") anticipates that the Taliban will insist on clarity that this article is not a large loophole in the foreign troop withdrawal provisions and that any follow-on foreign security force presence must be distinct from the current Resolute Support mission.

with Afghan authorities. The activities may include joint operations[19] against terrorist organizations and—to reinforce Afghan capabilities—training, equipping, and supplying of Afghan state forces reconstituted in accordance with Article II.6 that are engaged in counterterrorist operations.

C. Afghan Transitional Government and subsequent governance authorities may request additional states and organizations to contribute to or participate in activities of the Afghanistan Support Team at any time.[20]

D. To carry out any activities under this Article, the Afghanistan Support Team shall only use facilities located at Bagram and [*include any other agreed locations*][21] and any additional facilities as may be later authorized by the Transitional or subsequent authorities of Afghanistan.

E. Except as otherwise stated herein or subsequently agreed, any activities carried out by any U.S. personnel who may participate in the Afghanistan Support Team shall be governed by the Security and Defense Cooperation Agreement Between the United States of America and the Islamic Republic of Afghanistan (2014), and any activities carried out by any NATO personnel who may participate in the Afghanistan Support Team shall be governed by the Agreement between the North Atlantic Treaty Organization and the Islamic Republic of Afghanistan on the Status of NATO Forces and NATO Personnel Con-

---

19 One or both Afghan Parties might prefer specifying that only "joint" operations (i.e., operations involving Afghan personnel) will be permissible.

20 The Afghan Parties might wish to make such a request of one or more Muslim-majority states to make the presence of foreign forces in Afghanistan more palatable.

21 The number of bases and geographical locations probably would need to be negotiated and included in the Agreement to clarify the limited extent of the foreign military presence. Excluding the presence from Pashtun-majority areas might help gain Taliban agreement to the presence.

ducting Mutually Agreed NATO-led Activities in Afghanistan (2014).[22]

F. The duration of any activities under this Article shall be determined in accordance with decisions of the Transitional Government of Afghanistan or its successor.[23] The numbers of Afghanistan Support Team personnel engaged in any activities under this Article within Afghanistan shall be limited to levels strictly necessary to provide the requested assistance and shall be fully coordinated with the Transitional Government or its successor.

G. Upon the conclusion of any temporary and limited activities under this Article, the Afghanistan Support Team shall return to Afghan authorities all of the facilities and areas provided for its use in carrying out such activities.

H. The Joint Implementation Committee of the four Parties established in Part III of this Agreement shall be responsible for con-

---

[22] Unless an explicit reference such as this to the U.S.-Afghanistan bilateral security agreement and the NATO-Afghanistan status of forces agreement is included, the United States and NATO might consider it necessary to incorporate many additional provisions into this agreement, essentially replicating much of the technical contents of those two prior security agreements—if it is anticipated that U.S. and NATO personnel will participate in the Afghanistan Support Team. Renegotiating those provisions would be very burdensome. That said, it would be important to the conduct of Afghanistan's future foreign relations not to interpret an explicit reference to the two agreements as calling into question Afghanistan's automatically continued commitment to abiding by any and all agreements signed after 2001. An **alternative option** would be to eliminate explicit reference to the agreements, which are controversial for the Taliban:

> Except as otherwise stated herein, any activities carried out by U.S. personnel participating in the Afghanistan Support Team shall be governed by existing written agreements between the United States and Afghanistan, and any activities carried out by NATO personnel participating in the Afghanistan Support Team shall be governed by existing written agreements between NATO and Afghanistan.

[23] An **alternative option** could be to specify the duration (in months or years) of the Team and state that the time period could be extended by mutual agreement. This option might be preferable for the Taliban and for some regional countries if the specified duration was short.

sidering and resolving any issues related to implementation of this Article.

Article I.4

INTERNATIONAL SUPPORT FOR THE AFGHAN PEOPLE

A. Conclusion of this Agreement represents a historic opportunity for the Afghan people to experience peaceful life and build the social well-being and prosperity of their communities and their country. It is the intention[24] of the United States to support the Afghan people in fully realizing the potential benefits of this Agreement by continuing to provide financial assistance to Afghanistan for purposes of development. It is also the intention of the United States to provide financial assistance to the security forces of the sovereign state, if requested by Afghan authorities.[25]

B. The United States further commits to undertaking active efforts to urge other states and organizations in the international community to provide financial assistance in support of Afghan development and security, including by taking steps to ensure the organization of a donors conference to support implementation of this Agreement.

C. The United States also intends to offer to Afghanistan assistance with de-mining, removal of unexploded ordnance, and removal of potentially dangerous materials from former military facilities.

---

24 Because of the requirements of U.S. law and practice, in international agreements the United States can express intentions but not "commitments" to provide funding.

25 The current costs of Afghan security institutions are unaffordable by Afghanistan without foreign funding. Although conclusion and implementation of a peace agreement could be expected to reduce security costs, it is likely that Afghan resources alone would be insufficient to cover these costs for at least the near term.

Part II

Determined to ensure broad representation and inclusivity in the governance of Afghanistan at all levels and to reconstitute the state in a fully inclusive form,

Emphasizing their commitment to governance based on Islamic principles and Afghan cultural traditions,

Affirming the necessity of national reconciliation to achieving lasting peace, and

Recognizing the need for inclusive security institutions that reflect Afghanistan's diversity and protect its unity, independence, sovereignty, and territorial integrity,[26]

The Afghan Parties agree to the following:

Article II.1

NATURE OF THE STATE[27]

A. Afghanistan is and shall remain an Islamic state that is fully independent, sovereign, unitary, and indivisible. The sacred religion of Islam is the religion of Afghanistan. Followers of other faiths shall be free within the bounds of law to exercise and per-

---

26 The preambular sentences suggested here refer to some of the main principles and goals underlying the Articles in Part II of the Agreement; the Afghan Parties probably would wish to include additional preambular language, perhaps including religious and cultural references. .

27 Proposed language in this Article is drawn in part from Afghanistan's 2004 Constitution and also in part from research regarding Taliban views and interests.

form their religious rituals. No law shall contravene the tenets and principles of the holy religion of Islam in Afghanistan.[28]

B. The fundamental responsibilities of the state shall include

i. Upholding Islamic principles.[29]

ii. Safeguarding the values of Afghan culture and society and the ethical life of the Afghan people and promoting respect for Afghan traditions.

iii. Preserving public order and physical safety.

iv. Ensuring the welfare of the Afghan people.

v. Defending Afghanistan's independence, sovereignty, and territorial integrity.

vi. Conducting foreign and national security policy on the basis of noninterference, good neighborliness, mutual respect, neutrality,[30] and rejection of foreign influence.

---

28 This paragraph contains language substantially similar to the 2004 Constitution. The Taliban might argue for a stronger formulation in the new constitution, perhaps calling for all laws to be *based on* Islamic law.

29 An **alternative** could be "implementing Islam in all aspects of life."

30 **Alternatively**, "neutrality" could be excluded from this provision, but its inclusion might help attract the support of some regional states for this Agreement. A simple statement of "neutrality" such as this would not in reality return Afghanistan to its 19th- and early 20th-century status as a buffer state between great powers and would not deprive Afghanistan of independence in its foreign policy, but it would imply an intention not to take sides in regional hot or cold conflicts.

In Cambodia—a conflict context in which foreign states featured significantly—a status of "neutrality" was stated in the 1991 Paris Peace Agreements, including in the preamble ("In order to maintain, preserve and defend the sovereignty, independence, territorial integrity and inviolability, neutrality and national unity of Cambodia") and in provisions specifying language to be incorporated in the new constitution (Art. 23 and Annex 5.3).

vii. Operating all institutions of government based on the rule of law and with integrity and intolerance of corruption.

Article II.2

STATUS OF CONSTITUTION[31]

A. The Transitional Executive established in accordance with Article II.4 shall organize and oversee a process for adopting a new constitution of Afghanistan. Within twelve months of signature of this Agreement, a constitutional assembly shall be convened to adopt the new constitution.

B. The Transitional Executive shall appoint a committee to prepare a draft constitution for submission to the constitutional

---

For a review of neutrality as a pillar of Afghanistan's historical foreign policy and proposals to restore it, see Nasir A. Andisha, "Neutrality in Afghanistan's Foreign Policy," Washington, D.C.: U.S. Institute of Peace, March 2015.

[31] Constitutional reform or adoption of entirely new constitutions has featured in numerous peace processes at various stages, including, for example, in Bosnia, Cambodia, Colombia, Macedonia, the Philippines (2014 agreement with the Moro Islamic Liberation Front), and South Africa. These past experiences suggest that it would not be unusual, or problematic in terms of international practice, for Afghanistan to either modify or adopt a wholly new constitution as part of a peace process without applying the amendment provisions of the 2004 Constitution, which itself was adopted pursuant to the 2001 Bonn Agreement rather than any preexisting procedures in Afghan law.

The Transitional authorities will need to determine the composition of a constitutional assembly for adopting a new constitution; even if the parties could agree to use the procedures for calling a Constitutional Loya Jirga that are in the 2004 Constitution, those procedures cannot be implemented without holding District Council elections, which has never occurred. The constitutional assembly could resemble so-called "traditional" Loya Jirgas, several of which have been held in the post-2001 period and have been established on largely tribal, ethnic, and regional bases. If possible, determining the composition of a constitutional assembly in this Agreement rather than deferring the question to the Transitional authorities could improve prospects for implementation by removing one of many contentious decisions from those authorities' agenda.

assembly.[32] The new constitution shall be based on principles of Islam, human rights, and Afghan national values.[33]

C. The draft constitution prepared by the committee shall be consistent with the entirety of this Agreement, shall implement the provisions of this Agreement on governance in Article II.3, and shall specifically include the provisions of Article II.1 regarding the nature of the state and the fundamental duties of the state. The committee shall also give due regard to the text of the 2004 Constitution and, in the interests of both national reconciliation and practicality, shall utilize that text as the initial basis for preparing a new draft.[34]

D. The provisions on fundamental rights in the draft constitution submitted to the constitutional assembly shall include equal rights and duties for all citizens of Afghanistan and the rights of

---

32 **Alternative options** could include adding to the Agreement, probably in an annex, either the entire draft text of a new constitution, agreed modifications to the 2004 Constitution (if the Taliban agreed to amending the constitution rather than adopting a new one), or a list of specific constitutional provisions the parties agree will be discussed or altered. Any of these options could be combined with a commitment in the text of the Agreement to supporting in a constitutional assembly adoption of the agreed text or modifications, so that there would be a formal ratification procedure. These options would avoid shifting probably contentious debate over the terms of the constitution to the drafting committee and Transitional Government, which could impede implementation of the peace agreement but would add complexity to the peace negotiations. Variations of these options are featured in peace agreements for Bosnia, Macedonia, and South Africa, as discussed in Chapter Four.

33 This sentence is drawn from the statement of Taliban representatives at a Track II dialogue in Chantilly, France, in December 2012. As noted above, an **alternative** to "principles" of Islam could be "provisions and beliefs," as in the 2004 Constitution.

34 This provision attempts to balance several factors: the Taliban's insistence on a "new" constitution in light of their exclusion from the 2004 constitution-making process, the attachment of many Afghans to an existing constitution under which they have lived for many years, the probability that many, if not most, elements of the existing constitution will be unobjectionable to the Taliban, and the practical reality that writing a new constitution starting from a blank page would be practically burdensome and very time-consuming.

all citizens of Afghanistan to equal access to education, employment, and health care.[35]

E. Until adoption of the new constitution, the 2004 Constitution shall remain in effect on a transitional basis, except where in conflict with this Agreement.

F. The Afghan Parties commit to supporting the constitutional assembly's adoption of constitutional text that adheres to the provisions of this Article and is fully consistent with the entirety of this Agreement. The Afghan Parties further commit to implementation of the new constitution once it is adopted and to supporting the amendment of laws and adoption of new laws as needed to ensure consistency with the new constitution.

Article II.3[36]

[35] This provision, which adapts language from the 2004 Constitution, is intended to ensure the parties' commitment to a minimum standard for protection of human rights, including rights for women and minorities. It also builds on the Taliban's claimed disavowal of any ban on female education, notwithstanding the limitations in practice on education of females in Taliban-controlled areas. See Ashley Jackson, *Life Under the Taliban Shadow Government*, London: Overseas Development Institute, June 2018, pp. 14–15, regarding constraints on girls' education in both Taliban-controlled and government-controlled areas.

[36] An **alternative option** would be to exclude from this Agreement substantive provisions regarding new permanent governance arrangements for the post-transitional period and to specify instead that either the transitional governance bodies or some form of consultative inter-Afghan dialogue (perhaps a Loya Jirga) will debate and determine the new political system. This alternative approach might be favored by the Taliban and possibly by some elements of the Afghan government–associated political elite (particularly those who are not satisfied with the ideas under consideration during peace negotiations).

A more comprehensive and determinative approach is suggested here because **deferring such contentious and challenging issues could increase significantly the risk of prolonged transition and ultimately implementation failure.** Once the pressure of concluding a peace agreement is relieved, the incentives of the Afghan Parties to reach agreement on deferred issues would likely be reduced.

If permanent governance arrangements are entirely excluded from an Agreement or only addressed in brief outline form, the ideas presented here could be used to inform the subsequent dialogue on this topic.

GOVERNANCE[37]

A. The structure of government and exercise of governance authority throughout Afghanistan and at all levels shall be based on these principles:[38]

   i. At the national level, inclusion and equitable representation of the diversity of ethnic, tribal,[39] and religious communities of Afghanistan shall be ensured in all institutions of government.

---

37 See Chapter Four for a discussion of varied approaches to achieving inclusivity and distribution of power through governance arrangements. According to research and consultations for purposes of preparing this text, Afghans associated with both sides of the conflict appear to reject soundly the idea of numerical or percentage quota-based forms of inclusivity (or "power-sharing"), such as the distribution of power on an explicitly ethnic, tribal, geographic, or organizational identity basis. (Relatively extreme examples of this type of approach in other contexts include Lebanon and Bosnia.) Therefore, it is necessary to devise a governance structure that will, *in effect*, ensure equitable and broad-based distribution of power. This is difficult to do at the national level. One possible method would be to adopt a parliamentary system of government, perhaps with a party-list proportional representation electoral system and a requirement that the slate of ministers reflects the relative strength of parties in parliament. That option—discussed further in Chapter Four—is not proposed here because Afghanistan currently lacks well-developed political parties, which are needed to make such a system function effectively.

At the subnational level, broad distribution of power can be achieved through devolution of authority and somewhat increased local autonomy, particularly if ethnic or tribal groups are concentrated geographically. Devolution has the benefit of distributing power in ways that increase the likelihood that power will be exercised by those who are representative of (or at least connected to through shared identity) the people over whom they are exercising power. Devolution also has at least the theoretical potential to improve the effectiveness of government, so long as it is accompanied by sufficient distribution of financial resources and a state monopoly on force. In any devolution scenario, of course, some local authorities will govern more effectively than others.

38 Some of the terminology in this section is drawn from the 2001 Bonn Agreement, including "equitable representation of all ethnic and religious communities," "the ethnic, geographic and religious composition of Afghanistan," and "all segments of the Afghan population."

39 "Tribal" is included here because negotiation of the Agreement will probably have to contend with intra-Pashtun (among Pashtun tribal groups) as well as inter-ethnic rivalries.

ii. At provincial and local levels, government institutions and informal mechanisms operating with governance authority shall reflect the ethnic, tribal, and religious composition of the geographic areas they serve.

iii. Government decisionmaking at all levels and in all institutions shall respect the ethnic, tribal, geographic, and religious composition of Afghanistan and shall treat all segments of the Afghan population fairly and with regard for their values and rights.[40]

iv. Individuals associated with the Afghan Parties, including those who have fought in the conflict that is ended through this Agreement, shall be provided equitable opportunities for employment in civilian and security institutions of government.

v. Governance at all levels throughout Afghanistan shall operate with transparency and integrity in order to end corruption, which harms the Afghan people and wastes national resources that are needed to build peace and prosperity.[41]

vi. There shall be no taxation or imposition of fees for free movement of people and goods except by state authorities.[42]

vii. Economic development measures shall be aimed at helping free Afghanistan from the scourge of poppy production and illicit drugs trafficking, which the Parties denounce.

---

[40] The first two principles relate to the structure and staffing of government; this third principle relates to the substance of government decisions.

[41] This anti-corruption principle and the later one regarding narcotics production and trafficking are consistent with the stated views of parties on both sides of the conflict.

[42] This principle is aimed at ending the practice of conflict parties and factions financing themselves through extortion of money from traders and others among the population.

B. To implement the principles stated above in this Article, after the 18-month period of Transitional Government specified in Article II.4, government institutions at the national level shall be structured as follows:

i. Afghanistan shall have a President, who shall be the head of state and shall be elected by the people of Afghanistan.[43]

ii. The powers of the President shall include[44]
   a. Serving as the Commander in Chief of the armed forces of Afghanistan.

---

[43] This provision suggests, but does not require, direct election of the president, thus leaving room for debate during the constitution-writing about whether the president should be directly elected by the population or indirectly elected by the legislature or a consultative forum.

A presidential system is suggested here because it reflects Afghanistan's history of *de jure* centralized authority under a single paramount leader (despite, simultaneously, a history of *de facto* decentralized exercise of power) and because such a system appears to most closely reflect preferences on the part of constituencies on both sides of the conflict. There are, however, constituencies (predominantly non-Pashtun) that have expressed divergent preferences, including for a parliamentary system of government.

This text also proposes some ways to moderate the extraordinary degree to which power is concentrated in the presidency under the 2004 Constitution. In the context of implementing a peace agreement, the current winner-take-all presidential system would likely make it difficult to ensure that principles of inclusion and broad-based representation are consistently applied.

An **alternative option** could be to establish a semi-presidential system, with a directly elected president and a government accountable to the legislature. In such systems, a prime minister is commonly nominated by the president and confirmed by the legislature; ministers could be nominated either by the president or prime minister, or though consultation between the two. Many variants of the details would be possible, but the main purpose of this alternative would be to balance power between the executive and the legislature to a greater degree than in a presidential system and to ensure somewhat greater sharing of power.

Creating a parliamentary system could be another **alternative option**. A challenge to effectiveness of such a system in Afghanistan, however, is that political parties are underdeveloped.

[44] The main idea underlying this subsection is not to provide a complete list of presidential powers but to indicate important ways in which the powers would be limited as compared with the current system, while still maintaining a presidency with genuine authority. This proposal introduces more checks on presidential power and shifts away from the extremely strong winner-take-all character of the presidency under the 2004 Constitution.

b. Appointing Ministers, the Attorney General, the head of the Central Bank, the justices of the Supreme Court, ambassadors, and the head of the intelligence service, with the approval of the legislature.
c. Appointing and removing senior offices of the armed forces and intelligence service, in consultation with the three Vice Presidents.
d. Declaring and terminating states of emergency and declaring war, with the consent of the three Vice Presidents.[45]
e. Appointing Provincial Governors exclusively from lists of nominees, as specified in Article II.3.C.i.
f. Such other powers as may be assigned in the new constitution.

iii. The powers of the President shall not include
  a. Appointing Provincial Chiefs of Police, District Governors, or any other civilian or security government officials below the national level, except Provincial Governors in the manner specified in this Agreement. This would not preclude officials of the national-level government institutions being assigned to serve in locations around the country.
  b. Appointing any members of legislative bodies.[46]
  c. Appointing Deputy Ministers, who shall be selected by the Ministers.[47]

---

45 The requirements of "consent" of the Vice Presidents in this section and "consultation" in the preceding section are intended to provide a check on presidential power. "Consultation"—a soft check—is suggested with respect to key personnel decisions to prevent gridlock in important but relatively ordinary government decisionmaking. "Consent"—a hard check—is suggested here with respect to extraordinary and highly significant government decisionmaking.

46 Under the 2004 Constitution, the President appoints one-third of the members of the upper house of the National Assembly.

47 This provision is meant to address the problem in recent years within some ministries of Ministers and Deputy Ministers not working as coherent teams.

iv. There shall be three Vice Presidents.[48] For two consecutive elections, all electoral slates of a presidential and three vice-presidential candidates shall be required to be representative of Afghanistan's ethnic groups.[49]

v. The cabinet of Ministers shall at all times be fully inclusive and shall reflect the composition of Afghanistan. Individual Ministers must be professionally competent and persons of integrity.

vi. The legislature shall have two chambers.[50]

---

48 This is an increase from two under the 2004 Constitution; the intention is to create more space at the most senior level of government for representation of ethnic and tribal groups.

An **alternative option** could be four Vice Presidents, implicitly to create space for one each of the main ethnic groups (Pashtun, Uzbek, Tajik, and Hazara), in addition to the President likely being a Pashtun or potentially a Tajik.

Another **alternative option** could be to specify that the First Vice President shall be the individual who received the second greatest number of votes in the presidential election. The purpose of this provision would be to alleviate the risk of political crises stemming from fraud and close votes in presidential elections, as happened in 2014.

An **additional option** could be to specify (in this Agreement, or in the constitution) substantive duties for the Vice Presidents to increase the significance of their roles in governing. Increasing the number of Vice Presidents without assigning substantive duties to them might do little in terms of broadening the distribution of power. One possibility could be to give each Vice President some degree of oversight of a substantive policy area.

49 In the current system, this type of ethnic balancing has been the general practice in presidential elections; the purpose of this requirement would be to promote inclusion by ensuring that such a practice continues.

50 This text uses the generic term "legislature" so as not to pre-judge terminology that the Afghan parties might wish to use.

Improving the representativeness of the legislature, including through changes from the current system suggested in this text, could be one form of achieving greater inclusiveness at the national level of government, in particular because of the legislature's role in approving ministers.

An **additional option** to enhance power-sharing could be to add super-majority requirements for passing some types of or all legislation, but this option probably would add unnecessary complexity.

Under the 2004 Constitution, there are quotas for women in both houses of the National Assembly. This Agreement text does not specify such quotas (thus sidestepping an issue that

a. The members of the first chamber shall be elected from constituencies that correspond to the Districts of Afghanistan; there shall be one member from each constituency (each District). The Transitional Government shall consider whether District boundaries should be redrawn and the number of Districts reduced.[51]
b. The second chamber shall be composed of three members from each Province. Each Province shall determine how it selects its members.[52]
c. The electoral system for directly elected members of the legislature shall be based on the principle of representativeness. The electoral system used in recent years

---

probably would be contentious in peace negotiations) but also does not preclude including them in the new constitution.

[51] The current system for the lower house of the National Assembly has multimember constituencies with a number of members for each constituency that is supposed to be proportional to the constituency's population. The idea behind the proposal here is to simplify the elections system, circumvent the lack of accurate population data, and tighten the link between legislative representatives and specific geographical areas. However, one reviewer of this report cautioned that a similar system in the 1960s led to overrepresentation of Pashtuns.

Unless the number of districts is reduced, this proposal for single-member constituencies based on districts would increase the size of the legislature as compared with the current system, perhaps to an unwieldy extent. In addition, redrawing district boundaries might be necessary to avoid overrepresentation of Pashtuns because, as pointed out by one expert during research consultations, the eastern districts (where Pashtuns predominate) are smaller than in other regions and the northern countryside (where there are fewer Pashtuns) is more densely populated than most of the country.

[52] As compared with the system under the 2004 Constitution, this proposal makes the following changes: eliminates representatives of District Councils, which have never been formed because of overwhelming challenges in holding District Council elections; eliminates appointment of one-third of the members by the President to reduce somewhat the President's power relative to that of provincial authorities; provides for three members rather than one from each Province; and gives each province flexibility in determining how to choose its members.

The idea behind such flexibility is to avoid predetermining the structure of government in each province and to allow for variability to suit conditions in different parts of the country. This approach might be problematic in mixed-ethnicity provinces (or provinces with competing tribal groups), however, because it could enable the majority or plurality to exclude the minority or minorities from power.

(the single nontransferable vote system[53]) shall not be used because it has not adequately implemented that principle.[54]

vii. A High Council of Islamic Scholars shall be established.[55] The High Council's members shall be appointed by the President and three Vice Presidents based on consensus. Qualifications for serving as a member and the term of members shall be specified in the Constitution. The High Council shall determine its own internal decisionmaking procedures. The High Council shall have the following responsibilities:

a. Ensuring that the laws of Afghanistan do not contravene the tenets and principles of the holy religion of Islam. The High Council shall review all[56] legislation

---

53 Under the single nontransferable vote system, voters cast one vote for one candidate in multimember districts. The system has been widely criticized for leading to many wasted votes and results that are not as strongly representative of the electorate's preferences as possible.

54 The text could go further and specify a new electoral system, but negotiating a new system as part of the peace process probably would be too complex. There is risk, however, in leaving an issue that has already bedeviled Afghan governments to the transitional phase, when consensus on tough issues will be hard to achieve.

One possible electoral system that might suit circumstances in Afghanistan is ranked-order voting, which can ensure that, where there are multiple candidates, a person with low support does not win. In a ranked-order voting system, voters specify on the ballots their first, second, and lower preferences among candidates; the winner is the person receiving an absolute majority made up of first and lower-ranked votes. This ensures that the winner has broad support among the voters.

55 A body such as this might create space for Taliban leaders to occupy positions of some influence as an alternative to competing for political authority through electoral processes.

Ideas for this provision were drawn from a review of similar bodies in several Muslim-majority states.

A 2005 "Order of the Islamic Emirate of Afghanistan" that appeared to be a Taliban movement counterpoint to the 2004 Constitution established an Islamic Council, the members of which were appointed by the Amir and the responsibilities of which have both legislative and judicial characteristics.

56 An **alternative option** would be for legislation to be reviewed only upon request of the President rather than automatically.

passed by the legislature and provide an advisory opinion to the President prior to the President's signature.[57]

b. Advising the President and legislature and making recommendations to the national and provincial governments regarding laws and policies aimed at upholding Islamic principles and safeguarding the ethical life of the Afghan people.

viii. The government shall establish mechanisms to ensure the transparency of government finances and the integrity of all public servants and shall foster a culture of intolerance of corruption.[58]

C. Also to implement the principles stated above in this Article, government institutions at the Province and District levels shall be structured as follows:

i. Each province shall have a Governor who is appointed by the President from a list of at least three and no more than five nominees selected by the Provincial Council; for the first nominees after conclusion of this Agreement and prior to Provincial Council elections, a provincial assembly of

[57] An **alternative option**, likely to be preferred by the Taliban, would be to make the Council's opinion binding rather than advisory.

[58] Countering corruption is highlighted here because of the significant role that corruption has played in fueling conflict in Afghanistan and undermining development. Colombia's Final Agreement to End the Armed Conflict and Build a Stable and Lasting Peace (2016) is an example of a (very lengthy) agreement that includes many more detailed commitments to combatting corruption than the language suggested here. However, even in that case, the commitments are predominantly process-oriented (for example, commitments to establish strategies, procedures, and mechanisms).

elders shall select the nominees.[59] Governors shall be permitted to serve no more than two terms in office.[60]

ii. Each province shall have a directly elected Provincial Council.[61]

iii. The provincial governance authorities, composed of the Governor, officials appointed by the Governor, and the Provincial Council, shall have the following responsibilities in each province:[62]

---

59 The current systems for Afghan government selection of provincial governors and Taliban selection of "shadow" provincial governors bear more resemblance to each other than to this proposal. Both systems are highly centralized; the President of Afghanistan appoints provincial governors (a practice that is not, however, written into the 2004 Constitution), and the Taliban's leadership *shura* appoints "shadow" governors. In both cases, appointments are often made of individuals not from the province to which they are assigned. (Regarding the Taliban "shadow" governor system, see Jackson, 2018, p. 11; and Antonio Giustozzi, *Negotiating with the Taliban: Issues and Prospects*, New York: Century Foundation, 2010, pp. 19–21.)

Nevertheless, as discussed further in Chapter Four, devolution of some authority to the provincial level—which, to be meaningful, implies a strong local role in selecting provincial leadership—appears to be the most feasible means of ensuring broad-based distribution of power across ethnic and tribal groups and thus could be the minimally acceptable option that enjoys the greatest support from among the Afghan Parties and factions.

An **alternative option** could be to directly elect governors. Electing governors could risk reinforcing warlordism, but a system of appointed governors risks perpetuating the political instability that has been associated with an exceptionally powerful, winner-take-all presidency.

Another **alternative option** could be for provincial governors to be selected indirectly—either by a consultative mechanism, such as a *shura*, or by the provincial council—rather than directly elected or appointed by the President.

60 The purpose of limiting to two terms is to mitigate the risk of reinforcing warlordism that is inherent in strengthening the independence of provincial governors.

61 An **alternative option** could be that the provincial councils may be *either* directly elected or indirectly selected in accordance with procedures to be determined by a provincial consultative process. The rationale for this alternative would be to permit more regional diversity in accordance with local preferences. A weakness is that implementation of this option would be more complex.

62 By comparison, the 2004 Constitution provides that the central government shall "transfer necessary powers" to the provinces (Articles 136 and 137) but is otherwise silent on the

a. Establishing and overseeing police institutions and maintaining law and order in the province, in accordance with Article II.6 of this Agreement.[63]
b. Implementing national policies within the province.[64]
c. Communicating to the President, legislature, and ministers the views and needs of the provincial population.
d. Coordinating the implementation of policies within the districts of the province.
e. Ensuring that district governance authorities have adequate and equitably distributed financial resources for carrying out their responsibilities.
f. Such other responsibilities as may be specified in the new constitution.

iv. The President and national legislature shall ensure that adequate financial resources are distributed equitably to the provincial governance authorities to enable them to carry out their responsibilities.[65]

---

authorities of the provinces and lower levels of government.

63 Decentralization of policing would be a significant change as compared with the system under the 2004 Constitution. The main purpose of this provision is to provide a means of absorbing, regularizing, and connecting to the state as much as possible the array of militias, armed groups, and fighters that currently exist on both sides of the conflict. The premise underlying this provision is that it will not be realistic simply to call for the demobilization and disbandment of such groups.

64 The approach proposed here would give the provinces a role in shaping implementation of policies in all areas of government while still giving the central government responsibility for setting the main lines of policy. The idea of "implementation" responsibility is somewhat ambiguous, however. An **alternative option**—which would be clearer but probably more controversial and harder to negotiate—would be to divide policy areas of responsibility between the central and provincial levels of government (e.g., education at the provincial level, health care at the central level). This approach is not unusual, even in unitary states.

65 For any meaningful degree of decentralization to be effective, additional and more detailed arrangements in the constitution or in laws would be needed to ensure that the provinces have sufficient financial resources. This might be done by allowing provinces to impose certain types of taxes or by specifying percentage shares of national revenue to be distributed to provinces.

v. District governance authorities shall be selected in a manner and for positions determined by respected elders within each district. The district authorities may either be directly elected by the district's voters or indirectly chosen through a mechanism such as a districtwide *jirga*.[66]

vi. District governance authorities shall have the following responsibilities:
   a. Assisting provincial governance authorities in carrying out their duties.
   b. Communicating the views and needs of district populations to the provincial governance authorities.
   c. Such other responsibilities as may be delegated by provincial governance authorities or specified in the new constitution.
   d. Organizing payment of stipends funded by the central government for *Khatibs* [leaders of Friday prayers].[67]

vii. The Transitional Government shall consider whether to redraw provincial boundaries in order to reduce the number of provinces or to create several larger regions composed of several provinces each.[68] The Transitional Government

---

66 This proposal allows for variation to suit conditions in different areas of Afghanistan. It also reflects the reality that local elections are too costly and difficult to organize in many parts of the country. This reality is borne out by the fact that district and village council elections called for in the 2004 Constitution have, by 2018, never been held.

An **alternative option** could be to allow each provincial government (governor and council) to determine the organization and selection processes for district governance authorities within its province. This option would limit the ability of local populations to influence their local governance arrangements.

67 The purpose of this provision is to promote close connections between local authorities and local populations, with the goal of reinforcing social cohesion.

68 Redrawing boundaries to reduce the number of provinces might help ensure that the provincial populations align with ethnic and tribal demographics in a politically stable manner. Creating four or five regions to supplant provinces or combine provinces into larger units of government could have the additional benefit (for revenue generation purposes) of ensuring that each region has direct trade and transit relations with neighboring countries.

shall also consider whether to redraw district boundaries and reduce the number of districts.

D. The Judiciary shall be independent of executive and legislative authorities and shall be composed of a Supreme Court, appeals courts, and primary courts.[69]

i. Primary courts shall be organized by the provincial governance authorities.[70]

ii. The President shall appoint, for staggered terms, the members of the Supreme Court and the chief justice in consultation with the three Vice Presidents and with the approval of the second chamber of the legislature.[71]

---

[69] Including provisions related to the judiciary might be of particular importance to the Taliban, which, since the mid-2000s, have focused attention on providing their own brand of justice and dispute-resolution services in areas under their control or influence. The current Taliban shadow system comprises—with variation in different areas—three levels of courts: a supreme court probably based in Pakistan, provincial-level courts, and primary courts. Shadow district governors and provincial governors also play roles in managing and participating in the Taliban's justice system. See Jackson, 2018, pp. 18–19; and Antonio Giustozzi, Claudio Franco, and Adam Baczko, *Shadow Justice: How the Taliban Run Their Judiciary*, Kabul, Afghanistan: Integrity Watch Afghanistan, 2013.

Both the 2004 Constitution and the 2005 Taliban Order conceive of the judiciary as an independent branch of government.

[70] This provision is another element of limited decentralization and of allowing some regional variation. A provincial-level role in organizing courts does not exist in the 2004 Constitution system. An **alternative option**—a more modest change from the current system—could be to give provincial authorities a partial role in nominations and appointments to primary courts, while maintaining overall central control of those courts. It is not certain that the parties would agree to relax higher court appointment authority over lower courts to any degree.

[71] Consultation with the Vice Presidents is not required in the 2004 Constitution. A stronger **alternative option** would be to require "concurrence" or "consensus" rather than "consultation" for all the justices or for only the chief justice.

iii. The Supreme Court shall appoint judges of the appeals courts with the approval of the President, in consultation with the three Vice Presidents.[72]

E. The new constitution drafted in accordance with Article II.2 shall supplement the provisions in this Article with further details, as needed, but shall not contradict these provisions.

Article II.4

TRANSITIONAL GOVERNANCE

A. Upon signature of this Agreement, a Transitional Government shall be established composed of the structures and bodies set forth in the provisions of this Article. The Transitional Government shall be the sovereign authority of Afghanistan for the transitional period until the adoption of a new constitution in accordance with Article II.2 and until elections are held for the national-level positions specified in Article II.3.

B. The Transitional Government shall abide by the principles stated in Article II.3.A.

C. The foremost goal of the Transitional Government shall be achieving national unity and reconciliation.

D. At the national level, there shall be a Transitional Executive with the following structure and responsibilities:

i. The Transitional Executive shall be composed of [*specify number, depending on positions/names specified below*] mem-

---

72 Consultation with the Vice Presidents is not required in the 2004 Constitution. A stronger **alternative option** would be to require "concurrence" or "consensus" rather than "consultation."

bers, including a Chairman[73] and four Vice Chairmen.[74] Each member who is not Chairman or a Vice Chairman shall be responsible for administration of a Ministry during the transitional period.

ii. The individuals who shall serve as members are
   a. Chairman – [*name*]
   b. Vice Chairman – [*name*]
   c. Vice Chairman – [*name*]
   d. Vice Chairman – [*name*]
   e. Vice Chairman – [*name*]
   f. Member responsible for Ministry of [*specify ministry*] – [*name*]
   g. [*list positions and names for each additional member*][75]

---

73 The first-choice option should be to name a single individual to serve as Chairman for the entire transitional period. An inferior **alternative option**, if it proves impossible to reach agreement on a single individual, could be to use the following language in the text:

> The position of Chairman shall rotate during the transitional period among the individuals named below who are assigned the positions of Chairman and Vice Chairman, in the order listed below and for equal periods of time.

Rotating chairmanship has the disadvantage of weakening the leadership role of the Chairman and could heighten the risk of dysfunctionality of the Transitional Executive. However, reaching consensus on a single individual to serve in this role could be very difficult. The rotation approach, if it becomes necessary, might have the benefit of helping incentivize the parties to avoid becoming stuck in the transitional phase.

74 This provision would notionally include two Pashtuns (one of whom would be Taliban affiliated), a Tajik, an Uzbek, and a Hazara. An **alternative option** could be a Chairman plus three Vice Chairman, which notionally would make room for one Pashtun, a Tajik, an Uzbek, and a Hazara.

75 This proposed approach (listing members by name and their positions) is based on the Agreement on Provisional Arrangements in Afghanistan Pending the Re-Establishment of Permanent Government Institutions (2001 Bonn Agreement). A similar approach was also used by Afghanistan, unsuccessfully, in the Peshawar Accord (1992) and the Islamabad Accord (1993). There is risk of paralyzed decisionmaking under this approach to transitional governance in the Afghan context.

Unless the assignment of positions to specific individuals is negotiated prior to signing this Agreement, there is high risk that implementation of the Agreement will either fail or be significantly delayed because of the difficulty of reaching consensus on such assignments. As compared with the 2001 Bonn negotiations, there are now a greater number of groups and

iii. The duties of the Transitional Executive shall be
   a. Ensuring full implementation of this Agreement in order to establish peace and security.
   b. Overseeing drafting and adoption of a new constitution within 12 months of signature of this Agreement, in accordance with Article II.2.
   c. Organizing and overseeing elections for positions specified in Article II.3 to be held prior to the end of the 18-month transitional period.
   d. Directing and overseeing re-formation of security institutions.
   e. Conducting foreign relations.
   f. Carrying out essential responsibilities assigned to the President and Government in the existing constitutional rules that shall remain in effect until adoption of a new constitution.
   g. Such other duties specified in this Agreement.

iv. Members of the Transitional Executive shall endeavor to make all decisions[76] by consensus, including decisions on decrees that it may issue and decisions on replacements of any members who become incapacitated. Any decisions that cannot be made by consensus must be made by two-thirds of the members present and voting.[77]

---

powerful individuals to accommodate, and there is probably no person widely regarded as both "neutral" and authoritative to put at the helm.

Negotiating the percentage shares of positions for different groups is likely to be contentious. Two probable approximate contending positions could be 50 percent Afghan government–associated groups (current government and non-Taliban opposition) and 50 percent Taliban, versus one-third Afghan government–associated Pashtuns, one-third Taliban, and one-third non-Pashtun groups. Trade-offs will likely need to be negotiated between resolution of this issue and outcomes on other issues.

76 This wording leaves some ambiguity about what must be "decided" by the Transitional Executive and what can be decided by the Chairman and Vice Chairmen, and by individual members in "administering" their ministries.

77 A variety of decision rules could be considered. One **alternative option** could be that, where consensus is lacking, decisions must be made by a simple majority of the Transitional

v. The Chairman, in consultation with the three Vice Chairmen, shall call meetings of the Transitional Executive and set the agendas. The Chairman shall represent the Transitional Executive. The next Vice President in the rotation shall fulfill the Chairman's duties in the Chairman's absence.

vi. No member of the Transitional Executive may compete for any position in the elections that the Transitional Executive shall organize and oversee.[78]

E. The Transitional Executive shall appoint members of the Supreme Court for the transitional period.[79]

F. The Transitional Executive shall appoint a Transitional High Council of Islamic Scholars, which shall serve until such time as a new High Council of Islamic Scholars is established in accordance with Article II.3.B.vii. The Transitional High Council shall advise and make recommendations to all Transitional Government authorities regarding policies and decrees aimed at

---

Executive members, *including* at least three of the four Chairman/Vice Chairmen. The 2001 Bonn Agreement provided for the Interim Administration that decisions would be made by a majority of members present when consensus could not be achieved (Section III.B.1).

[78] The purpose of this provision is to avoid creating incentives to prolong the transitional phase and to avoid any conflicts of interest in how the elections are organized and conducted. Among examples of such a prohibition in other contexts are Tunisia after 2011 and the Accra Comprehensive Peace Agreement for Liberia (2003).

An **alternative option** could be to exclude this provision. Arguments against such a provision include that the most credible and competent leaders would be needed during what would likely be a difficult transition period. Also, the provision might not prevent the most powerful political actors from promoting weak candidates for the transition period and exerting influence over them in the background.

[79] This language does not preclude reappointment of some existing members of the Court but implies that the Taliban—because it will have representation in the Transitional Executive—will have a role in selecting members. Under existing legal rules that would remain in effect during the transition period, the Supreme Court plays an important role in selecting lower court judges.

upholding Islamic principles and safeguarding the ethical life of the Afghan people.

G. There shall be no national legislature during the transitional period until elections are held.[80]

H. During the transitional period, all existing deputy ministers and heads of other agencies and commissions shall be deemed to have resigned but shall remain in their positions in an acting capacity until replaced and may be considered for reappointment by the Transitional Executive.[81]

I. The Chairman and Vice Chairmen of the Transitional Executive shall by consensus appoint Transitional Governors and Transitional Police Chiefs for each province.

   i. Transitional Governors shall organize their own transitional provincial administrations.

   ii. Transitional Governors shall determine how to organize transitional administrations for each district within their provinces in consultation with respected elders from each district.

---

80 An **alternative option** would be to keep the existing legislature in place and add members selected by the Taliban; under that alternative, membership proportions and voting rules would need to be specified (for example, one-third Taliban and two-thirds existing members for the lower house, with a two-thirds or two-thirds plus one supermajority requirement for passing legislation).

Another **alternative option** would be to establish a Transitional Parliament, all of the members of which would be selected from the provinces or the districts through consultative processes.

A no-parliament option is suggested here to avoid overburdening the transitional period with too many difficult implementation requirements.

81 This provision is partly based on Art. XXI of the Accra Comprehensive Peace Agreement for Liberia (2003).

J. The Transitional Governors for all of the provinces shall form an Advisory Council with which the Transitional Executive shall consult on important decisions, particularly with respect to implementation of this Agreement.[82]

K. The Transitional Executive may decide to extend the 18-month transitional period, in exigent circumstances, on the basis of a three-fifths majority vote.[83]

Article II.5

TRANSITIONAL SECURITY RESPONSIBILITIES

A. Until the security institutions of Afghanistan are reconstituted on a unified and inclusive basis in accordance with Article II.6, the transitional measures for ensuring security and public order specified in this Article shall be in effect.

B. As of signature of this Agreement, the forces of each of the Afghan Parties (the Afghan National Security and Defense Forces and Taliban forces) shall be responsible for ensuring security and public order in the areas under their respective control as specified in the map annexed to this Agreement.[84]

---

[82] The purpose of this provision is to provide a soft check on executive power in the absence of a legislature during the transitional period.

[83] Art. 22 of the Rwandan Arusha Accords (1993) contains a similar provision.

[84] Negotiating security responsibility for contested areas, where "control" is unclear, changeable at different times of day, or otherwise disputed at the time the Agreement is concluded, will likely be particularly difficult. Special, individualized arrangements might be necessary for some areas where contestation of control is intense and risk of ceasefire violations, including revenge attacks, is high.

A **variation of the map-based option** would be to negotiate areas of transitional security responsibility on a district-by-district basis, with a list of districts under control of the respective parties annexed to the Agreement rather than a map.

An **alternative option** could be to simply state that the parties are responsible for areas under their control at the time of signature of the Agreement, thereby avoiding difficult negotiations on a map indicating which side is responsible for which areas. This alternative

This responsibility shall include ensuring safe passage for and preventing reprisals against civilians and former fighters. The forces of each Afghan Party shall only patrol in the areas designated to be under that Party's control and shall transit through other areas only in coordination with the other Party.

C. It is agreed that the map annexed to this Agreement is for temporary, practical, transitional security purposes only and shall not be understood or characterized by any party as signifying

---

could significantly increase the risk of conflicts developing over who is in control where, especially in areas that are still being contested at the time the negotiation is concluded.

Some elements of the Afghan parties on both sides might reject the mapping (or district list) approach on the basis that it could be seen as carving up Afghan territory. During consultations, views on whether a map should be negotiated varied but were not unified on any one side of the conflict. The difficulty of implementing transitional security arrangements *without* a map (or district list) appeared to be appreciated.

A **second alternative option** could be to form transitional joint units composed of forces from the two sides that would provide security throughout the country. This would likely be very difficult to organize and manage without significant assistance from a peacekeeping mission or other neutral body but might be feasible if attempted only in selected areas of the country. One example of agreements establishing joint or mixed units is the Agreement for Peace and Reconciliation in Mali Resulting from the Algiers Process (2015), Annex 2.

If there were to be a peacekeeping mission, a **third alternative option** could be for the Afghan Parties to declare their forces and locations to the mission. An example is the Ceasefire Agreement between the Transitional Government of Burundi and the Conseil National pour la Défense de la Démocratie-Forces pour la Défense de la Démocratie (2002), Annex 1. This would put the peacekeeping mission in the position of having to mediate disputes over conflicting claims of control.

Also if there were to be a peacekeeping mission, a **fourth alternative option** could be for forces of the two sides to remain garrisoned until such time as unified state security forces can be constituted. However, it is unlikely that a large enough peacekeeping mission could be stood up to make this option feasible. Another important limitation of this option is that forces of both sides likely will need to continue operations against ISIS-Khorasan and possibly other terrorist groups.

A **fifth alternative option**, which would greatly benefit from but not require a peacekeeping or similar international mission, could be to create provincial-level joint security commissions. A difficulty with this proposal is that the commissions might prove hard to establish quickly enough after an agreement is concluded (or after a ceasefire is concluded, if that occurs prior to final agreement) to ensure that the cessation of hostilities does not begin breaking down. Furthermore, decisions about the composition of the commissions could be contested, and the commissions themselves could become forums for contestation unless there is a neutral entity to help mediate disputes.

any permanent divisions of Afghanistan or otherwise used to undermine Afghanistan's unity and territorial integrity.

D. An 11-member Joint Military Commission shall be established, composed of the following members:

   i. Three representatives of each of the Afghan Parties.

   ii. Two representatives from other states invited by each Afghan Party.[85] The two invited representatives selected by each Afghan Party may be from one or two states, as decided by that Party. The states invited to provide representatives to the Commission will be expected to provide practical assistance and support for unification of Afghan security institutions.

   iii. The head of the Monitoring and Verification Team established in accordance with Article III.1.[86]

E. The Joint Military Commission's responsibilities shall include

   i. Developing plans, as necessary, for implementation of transitional security measures, subject to the approval of the Transitional Executive.

---

85 Many peace agreements include similar provisions inviting representatives of other states and international or regional organizations to participate in similar commissions. Examples include the General Peace Agreement for Mozambique (1992), Protocol IV; the Angola Bicesse Accords (1991); and the Global Peace Agreement for the Central African Republic (2008).

86 Alternatively, this individual could participate as an "observer"; however, having an odd number of Commission members could be useful in preventing deadlocks.

ii. Rapidly establishing a unified transitional command structure composed equally of military leadership from both of the Afghan Parties.[87]

iii. Reviewing and replacing, as necessary, leaders of security institutions at the national and provincial levels for the transitional period.

iv. Resolving disputes regarding areas under control and assisting, as necessary, in coordinating transit of forces across areas of control.

v. Coordinating security activities across multiple areas of control as needed to combat terrorist groups, such as ISIS-Khorasan.

vi. Liaising with U.S. and NATO forces during the phased withdrawal.

vii. Organizing and overseeing reconstitution of the security institutions of Afghanistan in accordance with Article II.6, subject to decisions of the Transitional Executive. This shall include evaluating needs for new or supplementary training and putting in place plans and procedures for providing such training.

viii. Identifying needs for support from the international community necessary to ensure effective reconstitution of the security institutions and managing the receipt of such support, subject to decisions of the Transitional Executive.

F. Any disputes that arise within the Joint Military Commission in the performance of its responsibilities shall be referred for

---

87 Negotiating as part of this Agreement, if possible, the specific composition of the unified command structure could help mitigate the risk of implementation failure.

resolution first to the Transitional Executive, and second, if necessary, to the Joint Implementation Commission established in Article III.3.

Article II.6

RECONSTITUTED SECURITY INSTITUTIONS[88]

A. By the conclusion of the transitional period, only armed groups explicitly authorized by the sovereign state of Afghanistan shall be permitted to remain in existence. All elements of the forces of the Afghan Parties and any other armed formations that are not unified in the reconstituted security institutions of Afghanistan shall be demobilized, disbanded, and deemed illegal.

B. The national army, air force, border police, and intelligence service must be symbols of the unity and cohesion of Afghanistan and guarantors of the stability of Afghan governance institutions. The mission of these national institutions shall be to defend Afghanistan's sovereignty and territorial integrity. These institutions shall be reconstituted during the transitional period on the basis of principles of inclusivity and representation of the composition of the Afghan population at all levels of the institutions.[89]

---

[88] Ideas and some wording for this Article were drawn from review of military "power-sharing" and integration provisions in nearly 200 agreements, based on searches in the University of Edinburgh Peace Agreements Database (PA-X); PA-X, *Peace Agreements Database and Access Tool, Version 1*, Edinburgh, Scotland: Political Settlements Research Programme, University of Edinburgh, 2017.

[89] Plans for implementation of this provision will require significantly more detail than is presented here. Among many issues to be considered would be at what level integration of existing Afghan government forces and Taliban forces should occur—that is, whether small units should be integrated or kept separate, at least for some period of time, with integration occurring instead at the brigade or battalion level. The latter could make implementation of integration easier but might keep the armed forces vulnerable to fracture.

C. The reconstituted security institutions at the national level shall be composed of the following, which at all levels shall be inclusive and equitably representative of the population of Afghanistan:[90]

i. A single national army.

ii. A single national air force.

iii. A single national border police.

iv. A single national intelligence service. Appointments of senior-level intelligence agency officials assigned to serve in the provinces shall be made in consultation with and with the consent of provincial governors.[91]

v. Such other specialized, high-capability policing units at the national level as may be authorized by the Transitional Executive or the permanent institutions of governance established in accordance with Article II.3.

D. Other police institutions shall be reconstituted at the provincial level, under the authority of the provincial governments.[92]

---

90 This proposed approach relies on implementation of principles of inclusion and representation. **Alternative approaches** used in other peace agreements for which implementation could be more easily verified could include specifying percentages of positions to be filled by each of the parties (and potentially by different ethnic or tribal groups or factions) or specifying numbers of positions to be filled by each. These approaches would likely be more difficult to negotiate and might be rejected by the parties on the grounds of being too overtly divisive. As an **alternative to the principle of representation**, one reviewer suggested a provision that affirmative recruitment efforts will be made among parts of the population who could not join the security forces during the war.

91 The purpose of this appointments provision is to build local trust in and cooperation with the intelligence agency.

92 It should be expected that members of existing armed formations and militias will be absorbed into provincial police forces and thereby regularized. Doing so could help promote stability by providing employment for former fighters.

These institutions shall be responsible for providing security and ensuring law and order for the populations within each province.

i. The Ministry of Interior shall set neutral and objective recruitment and training standards for police that shall emphasize integrity and professional competence.

ii. The Ministry of Interior shall assist every province in organizing training for police.

iii. No individuals shall be excluded from police service based on their affiliations during the conflict.

iv. The police force of each province shall equitably reflect the composition of the population of that province. Police personnel must live within the province in which they serve, so as to be closely connected to the population they serve.

v. The Minister of Interior shall be responsible for appointing a Chief of Police in each province, subject to the approval of the Provincial Governor.

E. The officer corps, noncommissioned officers, rank and file, and other personnel for the national-level security institutions shall be composed of individuals verified to be serving in the forces and formations of the Afghan Parties at the time of signature of this agreement.[93]

This proposal to devolve policing responsibility to the provincial level elicited widely divergent reactions during the consultations described in Chapter One. Some saw it as likely to reinforce warlordism, while others saw it as a helpful means of integrating fighters into state structures.

[93] If there were to be a peacekeeping mission or other neutral actor assisting with implementation of the Agreement, that body could play an important role in service verification and selection of personnel for the reconstituted, unified security institutions. Such a scenario

i. The United States and NATO shall assist the currently existing Afghan National Defense and Security Forces and the currently existing National Directorate of Security in verifying service of individuals, and that assistance shall be accepted.[94]

ii. Individuals associated with the Islamic Movement of the Afghan Taliban who wish to participate in the reconstituted national security institutions shall have their service verified by Taliban leadership, subject to final approval by the Joint Military Commission.[95]

F. Special attention shall be paid to rapidly achieving reconstitution of the officer corps[96] of the national security institutions in a manner that accurately reflects the composition of the population of Afghanistan and unifies former combatants.[97]

G. After reconstitution of unified national security institutions and decentralization of policing is completed, the relevant governance authorities shall

---

probably would also involve cantonment of forces, which is not feasible with the approach adopted in this Agreement.

94 The purpose of this provision is to reduce the risk of "ghost" soldiers and police being included in the personnel lists, as well as other forms of potential fraudulent filling of the lists. The current actual numbers of personnel are below authorized levels to a sufficient extent that unification probably will not enlarge total force levels.

95 An **alternative option** could be to exclude the Joint Military Commission's final approval responsibility. This approval provision is included to provide a safeguard against inflation of the number of purported fighters. However, it is uncertain how the Commission would have information available to it that could be used to challenge verification claims.

96 Rank harmonization is likely to be a challenging task during the reconstitution process.

97 As with the transitional security provisions, an **alternative option** could be to specify percentage or numerical quotas for different ethnic and tribal groups and factions.

i. Evaluate the need for new recruitment of personnel on a nondiscriminatory basis and in a manner intended to improve inclusiveness and representation.

ii. Develop plans for adjusting the sizes of the institutions, commensurate with Afghanistan's security needs and available financial resources.

H. The Afghan Parties acknowledge that, because of the difficult economic environment in Afghanistan especially due to conflict, successful implementation of this Article and Article II.5 will require financial support from the international community.

Article II. 7

STATUS OF FORMER COMBATANTS

A. All former combatants, regardless of their former affiliations, have the rights to personal security, safe passage to their communities and homes, and nonpersecution based on their status as former fighters. All security institutions in Afghanistan shall be responsible for protecting these rights.

B. All former combatants, regardless of their former affiliations, are entitled to livelihoods and social welfare services, including health care and education, on an equal basis with all other citizens of Afghanistan.

C. In the interests of social healing, reconciliation, and preventing the recurrence of conflict, the Afghan Parties shall take all necessary measures to promote mutual respect for all former combatants and mutual honor for the lives lost on all sides.

D. The Afghan Parties request the international community to provide financial support to enable the transition of former fighters to civilian life.

Article II.8

DISARMAMENT[98]

A. While transitional security arrangements specified in Article II.5 are in effect, the elements responsible for security and public order in areas under their control shall also be responsible for appropriate and safe storage of heavy weapons. They shall declare and report storage sites to the Monitoring and Verification Team established in Article III.1.

B. Heavy weapons shall be defined as all armored vehicles, all artillery 75 mm and above, all mortars 81 mm and above, and all weapons 20 mm and above that could be used against aircraft.[99]

C. Upon completion of reconstitution of unified national security institutions and the demobilization and disbandment of

---

98 This is a fairly weak disarmament provision. Obstacles to strengthening the provision include that (1) after the Agreement is concluded, operations will still be necessary at least against ISIS-Khorasan and potentially against spoilers, and (2) disarmament models in other agreements involve either one-sided disarmament of former anti-state elements handing over weapons to state forces and/or a peacekeeping or peace enforcement mission collecting weapons—circumstances that likely will not apply in Afghanistan. Without a neutral or trusted security guarantor, it seems highly unlikely that the Taliban would agree to one-sided disarmament.

99 This definition is drawn from the General Framework Agreement for Peace in Bosnia and Herzegovina (1995). Some other examples include "artillery, mortars and anti-tanks" (Arusha Peace and Reconciliation Agreement for Burundi, 2000); "heavy weapons like rocket launchers and mortars" (Pakistan, Swat Peace Accord, 2009); "All weapons shall be considered as heavy weapons except pistols, UZZI sub-machine guns, sub-machine guns, rifles, light machine-guns (6.25 mm), medium machine guns (7.62 mm) and general-purpose machine guns (7.62 mm)" (Rwandan Arusha Accords, 1993).

any remaining nonstate forces or formations, all heavy weapons shall be handed over to the reconstituted security institutions of the sovereign state.

Article II.9

DETAINEES

A. All prisoners and detainees held by the Afghan Parties on the basis of political or military activities in connection with the conflict ended through this Agreement shall be released unconditionally within two months[100] of the date of signature.

B. The Afghan Parties shall ensure that released prisoners and detainees will not join any illegal armed or terrorist group.

C. Prisoners or detainees affiliated with groups or organizations that do not commit to or maintain a complete and unequivocal ceasefire shall not benefit from release provisions.[101]

D. The Transitional Executive established in accordance with Article II.4 shall be responsible for implementing this Article, based on comprehensive lists made by the Afghan Parties of prisoners and detainees to whom this Article applies. The Afghan Parties request the International Committee of the Red Cross (ICRC) to assist in verifying releases and commit to cooperating fully with the ICRC. The Transitional Executive shall designate an inclusive team of representatives to work with the ICRC toward that end.[102]

---

[100] This time frame is similar to those in other peace agreements, which generally range from "immediate" to two months.

[101] This provision is drawn from the Northern Ireland Good Friday Agreement (1998).

[102] Many peace agreements include similar requests for assistance from the ICRC, including those for Angola (1991), Bosnia (1995), Cambodia (1991), Liberia (2003), and Mozambique (1992).

Article II.10

AMNESTY

To consolidate peace and promote national reconciliation, upon entry into force of this Agreement, the provisions of the National Reconciliation, General Amnesty, and National Stability Law (Official Gazette, 13 Qaus 1387, Serial No. 965), which already applies to others engaged in hostilities prior to establishment in 2001 of the Interim Administration, shall apply equally to members of the Taliban movement. In accordance with this Law and under this Agreement, Afghans engaged in hostilities since 2001 are guaranteed judicial immunity in regard to past political and military acts, except for claims of individuals against individuals based upon *haq-ul-abd* [rights of people] and individual criminal offenses.[103] The Parties note that the application of

---

[103] The referenced law (published in the official gazette on December 2, 2008) has been controversial because of the breadth of the amnesty it provides; however, it continues to be applicable law in Afghanistan. Article 3 of the law states

> (1) All political actions and hostile parties who were involved in a way or another in hostilities before establishing of the Interim Administration shall be included in the reconciliation and general amnesty program for the purpose of reconciliation among different segments of society, strengthening of peace and stability and starting of new life in the contemporary political history of Afghanistan, and enjoy all their legal rights and shall not be legally and judicially prosecuted. (2) Those individuals and groups who are still in opposition to the Islamic Republic of Afghanistan and cease enmity after the enforcement of this resolution and join the process of national reconciliation, and respect the Constitution and other laws and abide them shall enjoy the benefits of this resolution. (3) The provisions set forth in clause (1) and (2) of this article shall not affect the claims of individuals against individuals based upon Haqullabd (rights of people) and criminal offenses in respect of individual crimes.

The Agreement between the Government of the Islamic Republic of Afghanistan and Hizb-e Islami of Afghanistan (2016) also provides a broad amnesty in Article 11: "The Government of the Islamic Republic of Afghanistan will guarantee judicial immunity of the leader and members of Hizb-e Islami in regards to past political and military acts upon announcement and in accordance with this agreement."

These precedents and the fraught history of efforts to counter impunity in Afghanistan suggest that a broad amnesty is likely to be included in any peace agreement, even though broad amnesties do not comport with best international practice.

any amnesty provisions under Afghan law is subject to Afghanistan's international legal obligations.

Article II.11

RECONCILIATION[104]

A. The Afghan Parties honorably and in good faith participated in the peace process because of their grave concern that decades of conflict have inflicted great suffering on the people of Afghanistan and created divisions among Afghans. A fundamental goal of this Agreement is to create a basis for achieving national reconciliation. The Afghan Parties have reached compromises on their differences so that the divisions of the past can be healed, trust within society can be rebuilt, national unity can be strengthened, and peace can endure.

B. To establish long-term peace and stability, the Afghan Parties have determined that an approach to dealing with the past is needed and that it should respect the following principles:

---

[104] The intent behind this Article is to express the importance of reconciliation and set in motion a process for addressing the issue. It is also intended to provide some balance with the preceding Article on amnesty. The issue of reconciliation, or transitional justice, in Afghanistan is complex given the long period of sequential and overlapping conflicts, the multiplicity of types of likely human rights and international humanitarian law violations, and the varied actors involved. Reconciliation focused only on the period of conflict since 2001 is unlikely to be successful in repairing national unity and social cohesion. Because of these and other complexities, attempting to fully work out the details of reconciliation mechanisms in the course of negotiations on a peace agreement could risk overburdening the process.

Many peace agreements express commitment to achieving national reconciliation. Some also establish mechanisms for carrying out that commitment. The specificity of peace agreement provisions relating to such mechanisms varies greatly (for instance, with respect to the purposes, types of activities, and structures). The text suggested here is within the range of precedents. The text draws generally from a variety of examples and draws some specific ideas for wording from the Arusha Peace and Reconciliation Agreement for Burundi (2000), the Stormont House Agreement for Northern Ireland (2014), and the Annex on Normalization to the Framework Agreement on the Bangsamoro (FAB) (2014).

i. The suffering of victims should be acknowledged and addressed.

ii. The rule of law should be upheld.

iii. Human rights should be respected.

iv. Reconciliation should be promoted in ways that are balanced, transparent, and equitable.

v. Community-level reconciliation is essential and should be promoted in ways that reflect and respect local values and traditions; processes may vary in different communities.

C. To put these principles into practice, the Transitional Executive to be established in accordance with Article II.4 shall create a commission mandated to develop and implement a strategy for national reconciliation. The goals of the strategy shall include

i. Preventing future violence and suffering.

ii. Preventing future divisions among the Afghan people.

iii. Proposing measures to end impunity.

iv. Proposing policies to address victims' needs.

v. Proposing policies for education to promote peace, unity, and reconciliation.

vi. Proposing such other types of reconciliation measures as the commission decides would be beneficial to the Afghan people.

D. The commission shall have 11 members.[105] The composition of the commission shall be fully representative of the composition of Afghan society and shall include eminent persons, respected elders, and religious scholars.

E. The commission shall conduct its work for two years, after which the national-level governing authorities shall decide on continuation of the commission or establishment of other mechanisms for a continuing, long-term process of reconciliation.

F. The commission shall establish its own procedures, which it shall submit to the Transitional Government for approval. The commission shall endeavor to make its decisions by consensus.

G. The governing authorities of Afghanistan shall do their utmost to enable the commission to accomplish its mission without hindrance, and shall provide sufficient technical, financial, and material resources.

Article II.12

RETURN OF REFUGEES AND DISPLACED PERSONS[106]

---

[105] This number is borrowed from the Colombia agreement on a "Comprehensive System of Truth, Justice, Reparation, and Non-Repetition" (2015); this number is suggested only to indicate that there should be an odd rather than even number of members and that a smaller number is more pragmatic than a larger number if the commission is to work efficiently.

[106] Wording in this Article is drawn in part from agreements and documents relating to Afghanistan found in the University of Edinburgh Peace Agreements Database since the Islamabad Accord of 1993 (based on a database search for "groups: refugees/displaced persons"). Some ideas were also drawn from the General Framework Agreement for Peace in Bosnia and Herzegovina (1995) and the Agreement on a Comprehensive Political Settlement of the Cambodia Conflict (1991).

In its 2016 agreement with Hizb-e Islami, the Afghan government committed to the "provision of land for their shelter with other necessary services in Kabul and other provinces" for "Afghan refugees living in Nusrat Mina Camp and other refugees based in Pakistan and Iran." An expanded commitment to providing land would be impracticable given the large number of Afghan refugees (1.4 million registered by the UNHCR in Pakistan alone), and therefore such a commitment is not repeated here.

A. Refugees and displaced persons shall be entitled to return to any location in Afghanistan in safety and dignity and free from intimidation, discrimination, persecution, or coercion of any kind. The Afghan Parties are committed to creating the conditions conducive to voluntary, safe, and orderly return. Returning families or individuals shall have the right to choose their destinations within Afghanistan without interference.

B. National development programs shall have among their priorities assisting refugees and displaced persons returning to their communities and reestablishing their livelihoods.

C. The Afghan Parties request the United Nations High Commissioner for Refugees (UNHCR) to assist the Transitional Government and subsequent governing authorities in developing and implementing a plan for facilitating the voluntary, safe, and orderly return of refugees and displaced persons. The plan shall include provisions for monitoring, repatriation assistance on a nondiscriminatory basis for those in need, coordination with states that are currently sheltering Afghan refugees, and such other measures as deemed necessary.

Article II.13

LAND AND PROPERTY

A. The Afghan Parties recognize that disputes over land and property have been an important source of conflict in Afghanistan. They further recognize that the expected returns of refugees and displaced persons to their communities and homes may increase the number and significance of such disputes.

B. Such disputes must be resolved in compliance with principles including

   i. Respect for the fundamental right to property.

ii. The right to have property that was wrongfully taken restored, or to receive just compensation where restoration is not possible or desired.

iii. Fairness of access to common property resources, such as pasture lands, forests, and water.

iv. Equitable treatment of returnees and other citizens.

C. The Transitional Executive shall establish an inclusive commission that will design and propose to the permanent governance institutions effective mechanisms for conflict resolution regarding land use and possession of land and property in accordance with the principles stated above in Article II.13.B. These mechanisms shall be designed to involve communities in such conflict resolution. The commission shall pay particular attention to proposing ways to address Afghanistan's significant challenges related to lack of land ownership documentation.[107]

Article II.14

IMPLEMENTATION PROVISIONS

A. The Afghan Parties shall request regional neighbors and the international community to lend their full support to implementation of this Agreement. They shall insist that all financial and other material support for implementation be distributed transparently and equitably throughout Afghanistan so as to strengthen Afghanistan's national unity.

B. The Afghan Parties shall continuously urge any armed groups that do not subscribe to this Agreement to cease hostilities and

[107] Some ideas for this provision were drawn from the Final Agreement between the Government of Colombia and Revolutionary Armed Forces of Colombia (2016), though the land and property-related provisions in that agreement are much more detailed.

join in national reconciliation. All necessary measures shall be taken by the Transitional Government and subsequent governance authorities to protect the Afghan people from such groups.

C. Where there are any conflicts between existing Afghan laws and this Agreement, the provisions of this Agreement shall prevail.[108]

Part III: Final Provisions

Article III.1

REQUEST FOR IMPLEMENTATION ASSISTANCE; MONITORING AND VERIFICATION[109]

A. The four Parties request the Secretary-General of the United Nations to use his good offices[110] to assist the implementation of this Agreement by establishing a monitoring and verifica-

---

108 Prior examples of such "legal supremacy" provisions include the Burundian Arusha Accords (1993, II.II.15.2).

109 In past peace agreements in other contexts, monitoring and verification has been assigned to an international body, a body composed of the former belligerents, or a combination of the two. Afghanistan has past experience with failed ceasefire implementation and monitoring that relied predominantly on the conflict parties, with no international guarantor or peace enforcement mission. The Afghan Peace Accord ("Islamabad Accord") (1993) provided that "[a] Joint Commission comprising representatives of the Organization of the Islamic Conference and of all Afghan parties shall be formed to monitor the cease-fire and cessation of hostilities" and depended on an all-parties Defense Council to form a national army, collect heavy weapons, and ensure freedom of movement.

110 The reference to "good offices" is intended to make clear that a United Nations peacekeeping mission is not envisioned and that the Secretary-General can respond to this request under his own authority.

tion team. The mandate for the assistance requested under this Article shall derive from this Agreement.[111]

B. The four Parties request that the team report regularly to the four Parties on

   i. Compliance with the comprehensive ceasefire specified in Article I.1.

   ii. Progress by the Afghan Parties in implementing the milestones specified in Article I.2.[112]

   iii. The Afghan Parties' compliance with their commitment in Article I.1 to ensure the removal from Afghan territory of unauthorized foreign fighters and fulfill Afghanistan's obligation to ensure that international terrorist groups shall find no safe haven within Afghanistan.

C. The four Parties also request that the team report regularly to the United Nations Security Council in order to enhance awareness of implementation progress among supporters of Afghanistan and this Agreement within the international community.

D. The four Parties understand and expect that the team, in the performance of its duties, shall coordinate closely with the United Nations Special Representative of the Secretary-General in Afghanistan.[113]

---

[111] This provision is based on the nature of the mandate for the assistance requested of the United Nations Secretary-General in the Agreements on the Settlement of the Situation Relating to Afghanistan (1988). A Security Council mandate for the assistance would not be required.

[112] This second monitoring and verification task relates to steps required to be taken by the Afghan Parties in order to trigger the troop withdrawal phases.

[113] This provision indicates an expectation that a United Nations mission in Afghanistan would continue to exist. An **alternative option** could be to make the monitoring and verification team subordinate to the Special Representative of the Secretary-General. At a mini-

E. Any of the four Parties may request the team to investigate and report on claims of ceasefire breaches, including claims of violent reprisals against former combatants (or others associated with the sides in the conflict) based on their conduct during the conflict. The team may also receive reports of violations from the public.

F. Composition of the team is expected to be determined by the Secretary-General in consultation with the four Parties.[114] The Secretary-General may request that each of the four Parties provides a specified number of persons to serve as liaisons to the team; the four Parties agree to comply with any such request.[115]

G. The four Parties agree that the Secretary-General shall make arrangements with contributing states for personal security to be provided for the team members and shall cooperate fully in ensuring the team's security.[116]

---

mum, such a team should capitalize on the extensive monitoring experience of the United Nations Assistance Mission in Afghanistan.

114 Implicitly, the Parties can request and veto specific members (particular contributing states and particular individuals).

115 Including representatives of the parties as liaisons to the team, or actual members of the team, would provide transparency and could help build the parties' trust and confidence in the monitoring and verification mechanism. This could also help in facilitating the team's access to areas of the country and might improve the team's ability to resolve compliance issues before they escalate.

An **additional option** could be to include here a provision stating that "the four Parties request that the Secretary-General arrange for costs of the monitoring and verification team to be borne directly by the states that contribute team members." The purpose of such a provision would be to simplify and expedite formation of the team if any objections arise to financing the team through ordinary United Nations procedures, but this approach would be unusual and might limit participation.

116 Armed security and secure transportation will be needed for the team to conduct its work. In the absence of a peacekeeping mission and depending on the ground conditions at the time the Agreement is concluded, ensuring security for the team could be a significant challenge.

H. The four Parties shall provide their full support and cooperation to the monitoring and verification team, including enabling full freedom of movement throughout the territory of Afghanistan and responding promptly and fully to all requests by the team for information.

I. Members of the monitoring and verification team shall have granted to them by Afghanistan the relevant privileges and immunities provided for by the Convention on the Privileges and Immunities of the United Nations (1946).

Article III.2

REMOVAL OF SANCTIONS

A. Immediately upon signature of this Agreement, the Afghan Parties and the United States shall submit to the United Nations a request to remove all remaining sanctions[117] imposed on members of the Islamic Movement of the Afghan Taliban in connection with their membership in or activities related to the Taliban.[118] The United States also commits to removing U.S. sanctions against Taliban members imposed due to their membership in or activities related to the Taliban. This Article shall not apply to individuals who may be associated with the Taliban

---

[117] More precisely specifying the scope of sanctions removal could be possible by referring to specific relevant United Nations Security Council resolutions or by more generally requesting the end of the United Nations Security Council Resolution 1988 "regime as a whole"; however, there are multiple relevant resolutions that form the regime as a whole, and such an approach might be unnecessarily complicated. Moreover, the regime might need to remain in place if it is expected that there will be listed individuals who reject the Agreement and to whom Article III.2.B therefore applies. Regardless, a list of names of persons to be removed from sanctions lists will need to be agreed to prior to signing the Agreement.

[118] Procedures for sanctions delisting can be found on the United Nations Security Council website (United Nations Security Council, "Procedures for Delisting," webpage, undated). The language in this Article is predicated on an expectation that the parties would reach an understanding in the course of negotiations on a specific list of all those individuals eligible for delisting and would prepare a delisting request in advance of signing the Agreement.

but are subject to sanctions for reasons unrelated to their association with the Taliban.[119]

B. The request to the United Nations for sanctions removal and the U.S. commitment to sanctions removal shall not include any individuals who do not commit to supporting and personally adhering to the provisions of Article I.1 of this Agreement.

Article III.3

JOINT IMPLEMENTATION COMMISSION

A. A Joint Implementation Commission shall be established immediately upon signature[120] of this Agreement composed of five members from each of the two Afghan Parties, five members total representing the United States and NATO, the head of the Monitoring and Verification Team, and the United Nations Special Representative of the Secretary-General in Afghanistan, for a total of 17 members.

B. The primary duty of the Commission shall be to resolve any disputes regarding interpretation of this Agreement. The Commission shall make all decisions through dialogue and consensus.[121]

---

119 The Article would thus not apply, for instance, to sanctions imposed explicitly because of involvement in narcotics trafficking, even if the sanctioned individual happened to be associated in some way with the Taliban.

120 This provision anticipates that the parties will have selected their members in advance of signature.

121 A consensus requirement obviously risks deadlock, but alternatives are lacking in the absence of an empowered neutral arbiter, such as a head of a peacekeeping mission, as in other peace implementation contexts. One possibility could be to refer disputes to the United Nations Special Representative of the Secretary-General, but the United States probably would not agree to that.

C. The Commission shall operate for the duration of the period of the Transitional Government and shall then cease to operate unless extended by mutual agreement of the four Parties.

Article III.4

AMENDMENT

This Agreement may be amended with the written agreement of the Parties.[122]

Article III.5

CONTINUITY OF COMMITMENTS

The commitments and obligations of the Afghan Parties expressed in this Agreement shall automatically transfer to the Transitional Government established under Article II.4. Following signature of this Agreement, the authority of the Transitional Government shall take effect upon its explicit acknowledgment of this Agreement and acceptance of this Article.[123]

Article III.6

ENTRY INTO FORCE

---

[122] An **additional option** would be to add that the Transitional Government could modify the provisions in Part II. However, there would be a trade-off between the certainty of the Agreement and flexibility in changing it, and greater flexibility might weaken the parties' commitment.

[123] The purpose of this Article is to clarify accountability for implementation of the Agreement, considering that at least the Afghan government signatory will not continue to exist as such once the Agreement goes into effect and the Transitional Government is established. An **additional option** could be to negotiate a side agreement specifying the Afghan political groups that agree to be represented by the Afghan government's signing authority and bound by the terms of the Agreement. Such a side agreement could be important to ensuring that all groups whose consent to the Agreement is needed to ensure implementation are on board.

This Agreement enters into force upon signature.[124]

DONE at [*location of signature*] this [*day*] of [*month and year*] in the Dari, English, and Pashto languages, each text being equally authentic.

For the Islamic Republic of Afghanistan:[125]

For the Islamic Movement of the Afghan Taliban:

For the United States of America:

For the North Atlantic Treaty Organization:

124 Some of those consulted (and one peer reviewer) suggested that it might be impossible for the parties to agree on how to refer to each other in an agreement text because of mutual denials of legitimacy and suggested that an agreement should therefore have no signatures, at least not of entities rather than individuals. No signatures might be a possible **alternative option** but could be resisted by the Afghan parties, which might insist on the use of their own preferred names at the same time that they object to using the preferred names of others. We opted for the more normal practice in both domestic and international agreements of including a signature block.

125 An **additional option** could be to conclude a side agreement among all of the important pro-government Afghan political parties and factions stating that the government representative's signature on the Agreement is on behalf of all of them. Such an agreement could symbolize the achievement of a unified negotiating position on the pro-government side of the conflict, which will be essential to concluding a durable accord with the Taliban. Achieving that unity is one of the main challenges in the peace process.

Witnessed By[126]

For the People's Republic of China:

For the Republic of India:

For the Islamic Republic of Iran:

For the Islamic Republic of Pakistan:

For the Russian Federation:

---

[126] Witnessing has no legal effect but could symbolize support for the Agreement among states with significant influence over the situation in Afghanistan, including influence over the likelihood of successful implementation. The states listed here are those with the greatest potential either to promote or undermine implementation of the Agreement and those which have had long-standing links with various Afghan political-ethnic factions; their support will need to be gained throughout the negotiation process. Including these states as "witnesses" implies that, leading up to conclusion of the negotiations, they will have been consulted through diplomatic channels and given access to the Agreement text prior to the text being finalized. Witnessing does not imply a seat at the table as a full participant in peace negotiations.

An **additional option** could be to add to the list of witnesses the three Central Asian states that border Afghanistan (Turkmenistan, Uzbekistan, and Tajikistan), or all five Central Asian states (adding Kazakhstan and Kyrgyzstan). However, keeping the list limited to the five included here might emphasize the particular importance of those states' support.

Agreement Between the [Islamic Republic of Afghanistan][127] *and the Islamic Republic of Pakistan in Connection with the Agreement on a Comprehensive Settlement of the Conflict in Afghanistan*[128]

Desiring to improve their bilateral relations, promote good-neighborliness, and strengthen peace and security in their region,

Determined to do their utmost to ensure that the Agreement on a Comprehensive Settlement of the Conflict in Afghanistan is fully and successfully implemented,

Recognizing the historic opportunity this Agreement brings for the two countries to set their relations on a new and better path,

Convinced of their mutual interest in enabling the voluntary, safe, and dignified return of refugees from Pakistan to Afghanistan,

The parties have agreed as follows:

1. Relations between the parties shall be conducted at all times and unequivocally in compliance with the principles of noninterference and nonintervention in each other's affairs and respect for each other's sovereignty, independence, territorial integrity, and national unity.

---

[127] This is conceived as a state-to-state agreement, but it is uncertain whether, under the Agreement on a Comprehensive Settlement, the official name of the state of Afghanistan will remain the same as it is currently.

[128] This Agreement is *separate* from the main "Agreement on a Comprehensive Settlement," but it could be negotiated simultaneously and signed at the same time.

2. Each party shall refrain from the threat or use of force, directly or indirectly, in any form whatsoever so as to disrupt the other party's political, social, or economic order.
3. Each party shall ensure that its territory shall not be used by any state or nonstate entity in any manner that would cause insecurity or otherwise violate the sovereignty, independence, territorial integrity, and national unity of the other party.

4. Each party shall refrain from assisting or supporting in any manner whatsoever any groups or individuals that intend to harm the other party and shall cooperate fully with the other party in preventing or responding to harmful actions by such groups or individuals.

5. Each party shall refrain from making any agreements or arrangements with other states designed to interfere or intervene in the other party's affairs.

6. The parties recommit to cooperating closely in facilitating the voluntary repatriation from Pakistan of Afghan citizens in conditions of safety and dignity and their reintegration in Afghanistan. The parties request the United Nations High Commissioner for Refugees (UNHCR) to continue performing its supervisory role in facilitating and monitoring the voluntary repatriation of Afghan citizens and reaffirm their commitment to full cooperation with UNHCR.[129]

7. The parties recognize that inadequately regulated transit of persons between the two countries has fed insecurity, conflict, and illicit trafficking of narcotics and goods. They commit to devel-

[129] Some language in this paragraph is drawn from the Agreement Between the Government of the Islamic Republic of Pakistan, the Government of the Islamic Republic of Afghanistan, and the United Nations High Commissioner for Refugees Governing the Repatriation of Afghan Citizens Living in Pakistan (2007, subsequently extended).

oping effective mechanisms for regulating and managing such transit.[130]

8. The parties recommit to full implementation of the Afghanistan-Pakistan Action Plan for Peace and Solidarity (APAPPS), agreed in May 2018,[131] which includes practical mechanisms for improving bilateral relations.

This Agreement enters into force upon signature.

DONE at [*location of signature*] this [*day*] of [*month and year*] in the Dari, Pashto, and Urdu languages, each text being equally authentic.

For the Islamic Republic of Pakistan:

For [the Islamic Republic of Afghanistan]:

---

130 An additional provision could be added recommitting to full implementation of the Afghanistan-Pakistan Transit Trade Agreement (2010).

131 Including a reference to APAPPS here could indicate that it is supported by a broad range of Afghan political elements and by the current Pakistani government and elevate its status beyond a political understanding between two former governments. Other understandings reached between the two governments could also be referenced here.

Declaration of Supporting States in Connection with the Agreement on a Comprehensive Settlement of the Conflict in Afghanistan[132]

The Agreement on a Comprehensive Settlement of the Conflict in Afghanistan signed today represents a major milestone in Afghanistan's progress toward a more peaceful and prosperous future and a historic opportunity for the Afghan people to set aside the divisions of the past, achieve national reconciliation, and build a better future.

The states subscribing to this Declaration commend this achievement and are determined to support the Afghan people as they strive to enjoy security and prosperity after many years of conflict and suffering. We recognize that peace and stability in Afghanistan is essential for enduring peace and stability beyond Afghanistan's borders.

As important as today's milestone is, an agreement alone does not ensure peace. Afghans must lead in seizing the opportunity for peace that is now, after difficult negotiations, within their grasp. We commit to supporting them as they do so.

As part of that support, we reaffirm our unequivocal respect for Afghanistan's independence, sovereignty, territorial integrity, neutrality, and national unity. We will do our utmost to promote a regional

---

[132] Such a Declaration could be negotiated simultaneously with the preceding Agreements and signed at the same time. A declaration would not have the legal effect of an international agreement, but the diplomatic challenges of trying to negotiate a binding agreement among these states would likely be insurmountable.

Ideas and language used in this Declaration are drawn from multiple multilateral documents, including Kabul Declaration on Good-Neighbourly Relations, Kabul, Afghanistan, December 22, 2002; London Conference on Afghanistan Communiqué, Afghanistan and International Community: Commitments to Reforms and Renewed Partnership, London, December 4, 2014; Heart of Asia-Istanbul Process: Deepening Cooperation for Sustainable Security and Prosperity of the 'Heart of Asia' Region, Beijing, China, October 31, 2014; and Declaration of the Tashkent Conference on Afghanistan: Peace Process, Security Cooperation and Regional Connectivity, Tashkent, Uzbekistan, March 30, 2018.

consensus among Afghanistan and its neighbors in favor of mutual trust, cooperation, good-neighborly relations, and peaceful coexistence, and against interference in each other's affairs. We appreciate Afghanistan's commitment, expressed in the Agreement, to prevent any use of the territory or airspace of Afghanistan in any manner that threatens the security of any other state.

Effective implementation of the Agreement signed today will be essential for the peace and prosperity that it promises to be realized. This will first and foremost require selfless leadership in a spirit of cooperation and reconciliation on the part of Afghans. In implementing the Agreement, Afghans must also be supported by close regional and broader international cooperation on development, economic connectivity, and countering the scourge of narcotics,[133] which are key to enduring stability.

We intend our support to be both political and practical, recognizing the continued needs of the Afghan people for assistance, especially in the aftermath of conflict. We welcome and encourage the combined efforts of all members of the international community to help Afghanistan create an environment in which peace can be sustained from the community level to the national level.

We stress the importance of women's full and meaningful participation in achieving reconciliation and building peace, prosperity, and effective governance, and we pledge continued support for international efforts aimed at enabling such participation.[134]

We commend regional countries, in particular Pakistan and Iran, for their efforts in hosting millions of Afghans, in the spirit of good-neighborly relations, over the past several decades, and acknowledge the strain this has placed on them. The Agreement, if properly imple-

[133] Iran and Russia in particular are likely to request a reference to counternarcotics efforts.

[134] A passage such as this is likely to be very important to eliciting the financial support of major donor states.

mented, should enable the voluntary repatriation of refugees in a safe and dignified manner, with international support. It also should enable enhanced efforts to address the issue of irregular migration.[135] Afghanistan's recovery from war will benefit greatly from the return of her sons and daughters.

Afghanistan's economic integration with the other countries in the region will further contribute to lasting peace and stability. In light of the Agreement signed today, ongoing support for regional economic cooperation and connectivity must be sustained with even greater determination.

Although serious challenges lie ahead, Afghans and the international community can best honor the great sacrifices on all sides of the conflict by ensuring that implementation of today's Agreement succeeds.

For the People's Republic of China:

For the Republic of India:

For the Islamic Republic of Iran:[136]

For the Islamic Republic of Pakistan:

For the Russian Federation:

---

[135] A sentence such as this could be important to European donors.

[136] The signatories listed here would be especially important in light of their particular abilities to reinforce, or to undermine, implementation of the negotiated comprehensive settlement. Additional states that probably would be willing to sign on and whose political and financial support could also reinforce implementation would include

- the five Central Asian states (Kazakhstan, Kyrgyzstan, Tajikistan, Turkmenistan, Uzbekistan)
- Gulf states including Qatar, Saudi Arabia, and the United Arab Emirates
- Turkey
- the major European donor states and Japan.

CHAPTER FOUR

Drawing on Past Experience: Comparative Analysis of Peace Agreements

Introduction

This chapter examines how peace agreements from around the world have addressed the issues discussed in the previous chapter that we identified as the most important or contentious in the Afghan peace process. The purpose of our analysis of peace agreements was to find ideas and language to draw on and adapt for purposes of preparing our peace agreement in Chapter Three, not to find models to replicate in Afghanistan. In essence, we turned to the rest of the world for inspiration, rather than importation. In this introductory section of the chapter, we explain our choice of issues and agreements, our approach to the agreements, and our methodology.

Scope

The scope of our analysis was determined by our overarching goal of supporting the writing of a comprehensive peace agreement for Afghanistan. As a result, the scope was limited by two dimensions. First, we focused on key or tricky issues for Afghanistan and did not analyze every issue that might be included in our peace agreement. Our decisions about which issues to examine were based on our review of the literature on peacemaking in Afghanistan, discussions with country experts and relevant political and diplomatic actors, and the lead author's direct experience working on this subject matter in the U.S. government. Second, we focused on comprehensive peace agreements from the post–Cold War period.[1] However, when it was valuable to look at noncomprehensive agreements or agreements from earlier eras, we did not hesitate. Our intent was not to undertake a systematic analysis of peace agreements but to inform the drafting of an agreement for Afghanistan.[2]

Further shaping the contours of the analysis are three issues about which we remain agnostic. First, the analysis is not constrained by the regime type that produces—or is produced by—an agreement. We examined peace agreements reached by democracies and nondemocracies alike. Second, our analysis does not account for the overall success or failure of an agreement. As a result, we do not exclude agreements that collapsed, after which the parties returned to war—such as the 1993 Arusha Accords in Rwanda. We do, however, avoid specific ideas or clauses that are widely considered failures. Finally, we did not seek to identify conflicts or contexts that exactly matched Afghanistan.

---

1 Comprehensive agreements are defined by two criteria: "(1) the major parties in the conflict are involved in a negotiation process; and, (2) substantive issues underlying the dispute are included in the negotiation process." Madhav Joshi and John Darby, "Introducing the Peace Accords Matrix (PAM): A Database of Comprehensive Peace Agreements and Their Implementation, 1989–2007," *Peacebuilding*, Vol. 1, No. 2, 2013, p. 261.

2 For more-systematic studies of peace agreements, see, for example, Caroline A. Hartzell and Matthew Hoddie, "Institutionalizing Peace: Power Sharing and Post-Civil War Conflict Management," *American Journal of Political Science*, Vol. 47, No. 2, April 2003; Karl Derouen, Jr., Jenna Lea, and Peter Wallensteen, "The Duration of Civil War Peace Agreements," *Conflict Management and Peace Science*, Vol. 26, No. 4, September 2009; Michaela Mattes and Burcu Savun, "Fostering Peace After Civil War: Commitment Problems and Agreement Design," *International Studies Quarterly*, Vol. 53, No. 3, September 2009; Madhav Joshi and Jason Michael Quinn, "Is the Sum Greater than the Parts? The Terms of Civil War Peace Agreements and the Commitment Problem Revisited," *Negotiation Journal*, Vol. 31, No. 1, January 2015a; Madhav Joshi, Jason Michael Quinn, and Patrick M. Regan, "Annualized Implementation Data on Comprehensive Intrastate Peace Accords, 1989–2012," *Journal of Peace Research*, Vol. 52, No. 4, 2015; Aila M. Matanock, "Bullets for Ballots: Electoral Participation Provisions and Enduring Peace After Civil Conflict," *International Security*, Vol. 41, No. 4, Spring 2017; Madhav Joshi and Jason Michael Quinn, "Implementing the Peace: The Aggregate Implementation of Comprehensive Peace Agreements and Peace Duration After Intrastate Armed Conflict," *British Journal of Political Science*, Vol. 47, No. 4, October 2017; Madhav Joshi, SungYong Lee, and Roger Mac Ginty, "Built-In Safeguards and the Implementation of Civil War Peace Accords," *International Interactions*, Vol. 43, No. 6, 2017; and Nina Caspersen, *Peace Agreements: Finding Solutions to Intra-State Conflicts*, Cambridge, United Kingdom: Polity Press, 2017.

Thus, we did not compare Afghanistan's conflict and social, cultural, economic, and political conditions to those of other countries in the hope of finding other countries to serve as models. This would both limit our search for ideas and falsely assume that similar countries' agreements are necessarily suitable for Afghanistan. In all, our search was broad.

Methodology

These scoping conditions and motivating concerns pushed us toward a fairly flexible methodology. Our primary method was a close reading of peace agreements deemed relevant, interesting, or otherwise useful. To identify agreements, we used the Peace Accords Matrix (PAM) created by the Kroc Institute for International Peace Studies at the University of Notre Dame[3] and the Peace Agreements Database (PA-X) created by the Political Settlements Research Program at the University of Edinburgh.[4] The PAM database covers the 34 comprehensive intrastate peace agreements reached between 1989 and 2012, while PA-X covers more than 1,500 agreements reached in more than 140 intrastate and interstate peace processes between 1990 and 2015. In addition to including interstate agreements, PA-X includes all agreements (not only comprehensive ones), which explains why it contains many more cases than PAM.

The great benefit of both PAM and PA-X is that they code each agreement in their database for substantive provisions, such as disarmament, human rights, and federalism. This makes it possible to easily find all the agreements that include, for example, amnesty provisions. PAM codes 51 types of provisions that fall in six categories: ceasefire, institutions, security, rights, external arrangements, and other topics. PA-X codes 225 types of provisions that fall in 11 categories: groups, gender, state definition, governance, power-sharing, human rights and

---

3 PAM is introduced in Joshi and Darby, 2013, and is available online (Kroc Institute for International Peace Studies, "Peace Accords Matrix," webpage, 2015).

4 PA-X is introduced in Christine Bell and Sanja Badanjak, "Introducing PA-X: A New Peace Agreement Database and Dataset," *Journal of Peace Research*, Vol. 56, No. 3, 2019, and is available online (University of Edinburgh, "Peace Agreements Database," webpage, undated).

equality, justice sector reform, socioeconomic reconstruction, security sector, transitional justice, and implementation.[5] To supplement PAM and PA-X, particularly for the years before 1990 and after 2015, we relied on the United Nations Peacemaker's Peace Agreement Database.[6]

Once we selected the important and/or contentious issues we wanted to examine, we used the databases to identify the agreements with relevant provisions, ideas, or approaches. We then read the pertinent sections of the agreements and inductively looked for patterns. As noted above, we generally did not account for the local conditions that produced a provision, and thus they were compared in a decontextualized manner. While reviewing agreements, we identified additional issues to explore.

In addition to examining the text of agreements, we reviewed the secondary literature on relevant issues. We were primarily interested in other comparative studies of peace agreements, but we also consulted the secondary literature on specific accords, when necessary. Our use of the secondary literature was ad hoc and was not a comprehensive review of the literature on peace agreements.

How Previous Agreements Can Inform an Afghan Peace Agreement

This section presents analysis of how existing peace agreements have handled the core substantive issues identified in Chapter Two as well as several other issues that we considered potentially relevant for an Afghan peace agreement. All of the core issues are included here

---

[5] For details and definitions, see the PAM codebook (Madhav Joshi and Jason Michael Quinn, "Peace Accords Matrix Implementation Dataset (PAM_ID) Codebook," Version 1.5, updated July 29, 2015b) and the PA-X codebook (Christine Bell et al., *Peace Agreements Database and Dataset Codebook*, Version 1, Edinburgh, Scotland: University of Edinburgh, February 19, 2018.

[6] See United Nations, "Peace Agreements Database Search," webpage, undated. See also the Language of Peace tool (Lauterpacht Centre for International Law, "Language of Peace," Legal Tools for Peace-Making Project, Cambridge, United Kingdom: University of Cambridge, 2018).

except for transitional arrangements, which we handled differently in our research. We assessed that, for transitional political and security arrangements, Afghanistan would require sui generis solutions, so, rather than conducting focused comparative research, we first drafted those provisions and then checked formulations in past agreements for potentially useful refinements. Beyond the core issues, the topics we also researched—and ultimately touched on in our peace agreement—are transitional justice (specifically, amnesty and prisoner releases), and property and land disputes. We used this analysis to inform the drafting of our peace agreement text presented in Chapter Three. In addition to the primary comparative analyses presented in this chapter, we consulted existing peace agreements on narrower issues or discrete phrasing in the process of developing our peace agreement text presented in Chapter Three. These other issues and agreements are often cited in footnotes to our peace agreement text but are not discussed here.

Ceasefire and Cessation of Hostilities

Ceasefire provisions, for obvious reasons, are nearly universal in peace agreements. Yet even something as seemingly simple as declaring the end of violence comes in a variety of forms. The central source of variation is the length and amount of detail included in the language. Some ceasefire provisions are very short and matter of fact. Djibouti's 2000 Accord Cadre de Réforme et de Concorde Civile, for instance, declares simply, "The two parties shall suspend hostilities."[7] Afghanistan's (failed) 1993 Islamabad Accord states, "A cease-fire shall come into force with immediate effect." The only detail it adds is that "[a]fter the formation of the Cabinet, there shall be permanent cessation of hostilities."[8] Many other agreements, however, provide much more detail about what precisely is meant by the ceasefire. Bosnia's Dayton

---

[7] Government of the Republic of Djibouti and Front for the Restoration of Unity and Democracy, Agreement for Reform and Civil Concord, Djibouti, February 7, 2000, Clause 5.

[8] Islamic State of Afghanistan, Hizb-e Islami, et al., Afghan Peace Accord ("Islamabad Accord"), Islamabad, Pakistan, March 7, 1993, Art. 8.

Agreement announces the ceasefire and then defines what actions it prohibits:

> The Parties shall comply with the cessation of hostilities begun with the agreement of October 5, 1995 and shall continue to refrain from all offensive operations of any type against each other. An offensive operation in this case is an action that includes projecting forces or fire forward of a Party's own lines. Each Party shall ensure that all personnel and organizations with military capability under its control or within territory under its control, including armed civilian groups, national guards, army reserves, military police, and the Ministry of Internal Affairs Special Police (MUP) (hereinafter "Forces") comply with this Annex . . . . In carrying out the obligations set forth in paragraph 1, the Parties undertake, in particular, to cease the firing of all weapons and explosive devices except as authorized by this Annex. The Parties shall not place any additional minefields, barriers, or protective obstacles. They shall not engage in patrolling, ground or air reconnaissance forward of their own force positions, or into the Zones of Separation as provided for in Article IV below, without IFOR [NATO-led Implementation Force] approval . . . . The Parties shall strictly avoid committing any reprisals, counter-attacks, or any unilateral actions in response to violations of this Annex by another Party. The Parties shall respond to alleged violations of the provisions of this Annex through the procedures provided in Article VIII.[9]

El Salvador's Chapultepec Agreement likewise details the specifics of the ceasefire:

> 1. The cessation of the armed conflict (hereinafter referred to as the CAC) is a brief, dynamic and irreversible process of predetermined duration which must be implemented throughout the national territory of El Salvador. During the CAC, there shall be no substantive negotiations but only the measures necessary to

[9] Republic of Bosnia and Herzegovina, Republic of Croatia, and Federal Republic of Yugoslavia, General Framework Agreement for Peace in Bosnia and Herzegovina ("Dayton Agreement"), Paris, France, December 14, 1995, Annex 1-A, Art. II, paras. 1, 2, and 5.

put into practice the agreements reached during the negotiating process.

2. The CAC shall begin on 1 February 1992 (hereinafter referred to as D-Day) and shall be completed on 31 October 1992.

3. The CAC consists of four elements, as defined herein:

a. The cease-fire;
b. The separation of forces;
c. The end of the military structure of FMLN [Farabundo Marti National Liberation Front] and the reintegration of its members, within a framework of full legality, into the civil, political and institutional life of the country;
d. United Nations verification of all the above mentioned activities.

4. The cease-fire shall enter into force officially on D-Day.

5. As of that date, each of the parties shall, as appropriate, refrain from carrying out any hostile act or operation by means of forces or individuals under its control, meaning that neither party shall carry out any kind of attack by land, sea or air, organize patrols or offensive maneuvers, occupy new positions, lay mines, interfere with military communications or carry out any kind of reconnaissance operations, acts of sabotage or any other military activity which, in the opinion of ONUSAL [United Nations Observer Mission in El Salvador], might violate the cease- fire, or any act that infringes the rights of the civilian population.

6. Official verification of compliance with the undertaking described in the preceding paragraph shall begin on D-Day. Any alleged violation of the cease-fire shall be investigated by ONUSAL.

7. During the period between the signing of this Agreement and D-Day, the two parties shall observe an informal cease-fire under which they undertake not to carry out any of the activities described in paragraph 5.

> 8. ONUSAL shall deploy its personnel and equipment during the informal cease-fire period, so as to be able to verify all aspects of the CAC as of D-Day.[10]

The complexity displayed in Bosnia and El Salvador is more common than the brief calls for ceasefire found in the Djibouti and Afghanistan examples. This is especially the case because many agreements include details about ceasefire monitoring and verification. However, variation in the text of the ceasefire provision itself appears rather idiosyncratic.

Foreign Military Presence

A central issue that will have to be resolved in the Afghan peace process is the future role of U.S. and NATO troops. Recent studies of Taliban leadership and foot soldiers find that one of the few absolute requirements for a peace deal from the Taliban perspective is the complete withdrawal of all foreign troops from Afghanistan.[11] Analyst Borhan Osman concludes that, for the Taliban, "No talks on other issues [are] possible . . . until the full withdrawal of the foreign troops [is] settled."[12] The Afghan government, however, depends on coalition forces for its survival and will demand that they stay for as lengthy a period of time as possible. This dispute over the presence of foreign troops means that negotiators will likely need to agree on the pace, scope, and conditions for a foreign troop withdrawal, as well as the means for monitoring and verifying implementation of these and related agreement provisions.

Other negotiators have wrestled with similar issues and reached compromises acceptable to both sides. As will be explained below, troop withdrawal is an issue for which we had to look beyond the set

---

10 Government of El Salvador and Farabundo Martí National Liberation Front, Chapultepec Peace Agreement, Mexico City, Mexico, January 16, 1992, Ch. VII, Arts. 1–8.

11 Osman and Gopal, 2016; and Borhan Osman, *A Negotiated End to the Afghan Conflict: The Taliban's Perspective*, Washington, D.C.: U.S. Institute of Peace, 2018. Stakeholder consultations by the authors suggest that this demand might not be as absolute as is often portrayed but that it is unlikely that the Taliban could formally and openly agree to anything less than complete withdrawal.

12 Osman, 2018, p. 19.

of post–Cold War negotiated settlements to civil wars. The agreements from the post–Cold War cases were less relevant to Afghanistan than agreements marking decolonization or ending military occupations by major powers or regional powers. We sought prior agreements involving the United States in particular, since understanding what the United States has agreed to in the past could illuminate what it might be willing to agree to in the future.

These agreements cover five aspects of troop withdrawal that are relevant to Afghanistan: the timing of withdrawal, specifications of what is to be withdrawn, steps for withdrawal, monitoring and verification, and options for maintaining a foreign military presence in the country.

Timing of Withdrawal

In the agreements reviewed, the withdrawal of foreign troops is generally given a specific, unconditional timeline. The agreed length of time for withdrawal, however, varies considerably. On the short end, South African forces were given five days to begin their withdrawal from Angola and it was to be complete in less than one month.[13] The United States agreed to 60 days to complete "a total withdrawal" from Vietnam.[14] And Allied occupation forces in post–World War II Japan and Austria each had 90 days to depart.[15] Similarly, the 1988 Geneva

[13] Government of the People's Republic of Angola, Government of the Republic of Cuba, and Government of the Republic of South Africa, Protocol of Geneva, Geneva, Switzerland, August 5, 1988, para. 4.

[14] United States of America, Democratic Republic of Vietnam, Provisional Revolutionary Government of South Vietnam, and Republic of Vietnam, Agreement on Ending the War and Restoring Peace in Viet Nam ("Paris Peace Accords"), Paris, France, January 27, 1973, Ch. II, Art. 5.

[15] Argentina, Australia, Belgium, et al., Treaty of Peace with Japan, San Francisco, Calif., September 8, 1951, Ch. III, Art. 6 (a); and Union of Soviet Socialist Republics, United Kingdom of Great Britain and Northern Ireland, United States of America, France, and Austria, State Treaty for the Re-Establishment of an Independent and Democratic Austria, Vienna, Austria, May 15, 1955, Part III, Art. 20, para. 3. The Austrian State Treaty caveated the 90-day timeline with the clause "and in so far as possible not later than 31st December, 1955." Given that the treaty came into effect on July 27, 1955, this caveat suggests that they had an additional two-month grace period.

Accords provided for a "phased withdrawal" of Soviet troops from Afghanistan to be completed within nine months.[16]

On the longer end of the spectrum, foreign forces have had two to three years to evacuate the country in question. Cuba had 2.5 years for the "phased and total withdrawal to Cuba" of troops in Angola.[17] The Israeli withdrawal from the Sinai Peninsula was to take place within three years but with specific, geographically defined phases. First, Israel had nine months to retreat "behind the line from east of El-Arish to Ras Mohammed as delineated on Map 2," and then it had the remaining time to move "behind the international boundary" between Israel and Egypt.[18] Finally, the United States agreed in 2008 "to withdraw from all Iraqi territory" in just over three years ("no later than December 31, 2011"). Before the full withdrawal, though, U.S. combat forces had approximately seven months to "withdraw from Iraqi cities, villages, and localities."[19]

Two agreements do not provide a specific time for withdrawal, leaving the pace undefined. In the Good Friday Agreement, the British government only committed to "make progress toward the objective of as early a return as possible to normal security arrangements in

---

16 Republic of Afghanistan and Islamic Republic of Pakistan, Agreement on the Interrelationships for the Settlement of the Situation Relating to Afghanistan, Geneva, Switzerland, April 14, 1988b, para. 5. This Agreement was part of the package of instruments that formed the 1988 Geneva Accords ending the Soviet Union's intervention in Afghanistan.

17 Government of the People's Republic of Angola and Government of the Republic of Cuba, Agreement on the Conclusions of the Internationalist Mission of the Cuban Military Contingent, New York, December 22, 1988, Art. 1. Cuba's withdrawal from Angola is the only agreement timeline that is subject to explicit conditions: Angola and Cuba "reserve the right to modify or alter their obligations" regarding Cuban withdrawal "in the event that flagrant violations of the tripartite agreement are verified" (Art. 2).

18 Government of the Arab Republic of Egypt and the Government of the State of Israel, Peace Treaty Between Israel and Egypt, Washington, D.C., March 26, 1979, Annex I, Art. I, Sec. 3 (a) and (b).

19 United States of America and the Republic of Iraq, Agreement on the Withdrawal of United States Forces from Iraq and the Organization of Their Activities During Their Temporary Presence in Iraq ("U.S.–Iraq Status of Forces Agreement"), Baghdad, Iraq, November 17, 2008a, Art. 24, paras. 1 and 2.

Northern Ireland."[20] And the Tripartite Agreement merely states, "All military forces of the Republic of South Africa shall depart Namibia in accordance with UNSCR [United Nations Security Council Resolution] 435/78."[21]

What Is to Be Withdrawn

All the studied agreements except one provide broad and general descriptions of what the foreign power is supposed to withdraw. The exception is the Paris Peace Accords, in which the United States agreed to

> a total withdrawal from South Vietnam of troops, military advisers, and military personnel, including technical military personnel and military personnel associated with the pacification program, armaments, munitions, and war material of the United States and those of the other foreign countries mentioned in Article 3 (a). Advisers from the abovementioned countries to all paramilitary organizations and the police force will also be withdrawn.[22]

The agreement also specified the "dismantlement of all military bases in South Vietnam of the United States and of the other foreign countries mentioned in Article 3 (a)."[23]

This level of specificity is not found in the other agreements. Their discussions of troop withdrawal remain far less detailed. Rather, they require the withdrawal of, for example, "[a]ll the United States Forces" and "[a]ll United States combat forces," "[a]ll occupation forces of the Allied Powers," and "the Armed Forces deployed in Northern Ireland"

---

20 Agreement Reached in the Multi-Party Negotiations ("Good Friday Agreement" or "Belfast Agreement"), Belfast, United Kingdom, April 10, 1998, Security, para. 2.

21 People's Republic of Angola, Republic of Cuba, and Republic of South Africa, Agreement Among the People's Republic of Angola, the Republic of Cuba, and the Republic of South Africa ("Tripartite Agreement"), New York, December 22, 1988, para. 2. United Nations Security Council Resolution 435 (September 29, 1978) also does not specify a time for the withdrawal.

22 Paris Peace Accords, 1973, Ch. II, Arts. 5 and 6.

23 Paris Peace Accords, 1973, Ch. II, Arts. 5 and 6.

and "security installations."[24] The 1988 Geneva Accords simply refers to "foreign troops."[25]

Steps for Withdrawal

Most of the agreements stick to the basic formula stating that "foreign troops must withdraw by a certain time" and do not detail what is supposed to happen between the date the treaty goes into effect and the date that the last foreign soldier exits. The troops are given a deadline for departure, but the time until then is left unplanned by the negotiators. However, several do specify interim steps to be completed before full withdrawal; specifically, they call for partial or phased withdrawals. There are two types of partial withdrawals that lead toward full withdrawals: (1) phased reductions in the number of foreign troops and (2) limits to the geographic scope of the foreign troops. Both forms of limitations can be either specific or general. France and Algeria agreed that the complete withdrawal of French troops would be preceded by a specific numeric limit to the French presence: "French forces . . . will gradually be reduced as of the cease fire . . . to 80,000 men within a period of 12 months."[26] The United States and the United Kingdom, however, did not provide a numeric limit in their commitments to troop reductions in the lead-up to full withdrawals in Iraq and Northern Ireland, respectively. The United States agreed to "reduce the number of the United States Forces during the periods of time that have been determined" and the United Kingdom agreed to "the reduction of the numbers and role of the Armed Forces deployed in Northern Ireland to levels compatible with a normal peaceful society."[27] Neither state gave a measurable benchmark.

---

24 U.S.–Iraq Status of Forces Agreement, 2008a, Art. 24, paras. 1 and 2; Treaty of Peace with Japan, 1951, Ch. III, Art. 6 (a); and Good Friday Agreement, 1998, Security, para. 2 (i) and (ii).

25 Agreement on the Interrelationships for the Settlement of the Situation Relating to Afghanistan, 1988b, paras. 5–6.

26 Government of the French Republic and the Algerian National Liberation Front, Évian Accords, Évian, France, March 18, 1962, Ch. 3.

27 U.S.–Iraq Status of Forces Agreement, 2008a, Art. 24, para. 5; and Good Friday Agreement, 1998, Security, para. 2 (i).

The United States similarly did not define the geographic constraints on remaining U.S. troops in Iraq. Rather, the United States and Iraq left the decision for the future, deciding that they "shall agree on the locations where the United States Forces will be present."[28] By contrast, the Israeli-Egyptian agreement supplied great geographic detail on the planned withdrawal. In particular, the agreement's Annex I, "Protocol Concerning Israeli Withdrawal and Security Agreements," and the Appendix to Annex I, especially Article II, provide detailed geographic limits that define the phased Israeli withdrawal and phased Egyptian reclamation of territory.[29]

Monitoring and Verification of Withdrawal

There are two main models of monitoring and verification regimes for the withdrawal of foreign troops: (1) bodies made up of the former belligerents and (2) international bodies. The Paris Agreement ending the Vietnam War had both. The agreement established both the Four-Party Joint Military Commission (with representatives from the United States, North Vietnam, South Vietnam, and the Provisional Revolutionary Government of the Republic of South Vietnam) and the International Commission of Control and Supervision (with representatives from Canada, Hungary, Indonesia, and Poland, i.e., two communist and two noncommunist countries).[30]

The Israel-Egypt treaty entrusted Israel and Egypt themselves with the authority to monitor and verify the withdrawal of Israeli forces with the establishment of a Joint Commission "composed of representatives of each Party headed by senior officers."[31] The Joint Commission's purpose was "to supervise and coordinate movements and schedules during the withdrawal, and to adjust plans and timetables as necessary within the limits established by paragraph 3, above."[32] However, this agreement also had a role for the United Nations in the pro-

---

28 U.S.–Iraq Status of Forces Agreement, 2008a, Art. 24, para. 5.

29 Peace Treaty Between Israel and Egypt, 1979, Annex I and Appendix to Annex I.

30 Paris Peace Accords, 1973, Ch. VI, Arts. 16 and 18.

31 Peace Treaty Between Israel and Egypt, 1979, Appendix to Annex I, Art. IV, Sec. 2.

32 Peace Treaty Between Israel and Egypt, 1979, Annex I, Art. I, Sec. 4.

cess. After withdrawal, the United Nations would step in and provide a buffer between Israeli and Egyptian troops. Only after a week of United Nations deployment would Egyptian troops be permitted to move into the evacuated areas.[33] The use of the United Nations as a temporary buffer between the parties went beyond mere monitoring and verification of withdrawal but was related to that task.

Finally, the various agreements between Angola, Cuba, and South Africa call for the United Nations to verify troop withdrawal. As formally "request[ed]" by Angola and Cuba in their bilateral agreement, "Both Parties, through the Secretary-General of the United Nations, request the Security Council to carry out verification of the redeployment and the phased and total withdrawal of the Cuban troops."[34]

The Option to Maintain a Foreign Military Presence

Several of the agreements examined contain provisions related to some future role for a foreign military in the country. These are unique to agreements in which a regional or global major power is a party. None of the agreements for conflicts that lack major power intervention discussed below include the option for a continued presence of foreign troops, but it is unsurprising that regional or global powers are able to gain this concession. France, for instance, negotiated the ability to maintain some French forces in two of its former colonies: Algeria and Indochina. In independent Algeria, France retained control of one specified military base as well as other unnamed sites. As the Évian Accords state, "Algeria shall lease to France the use of the Mers-el-Kébir base for a fifteen-year period, which may be renewed by agreement between the two countries; Algeria shall also grant France the use of a number of military airfields, the terrains, sites and installations necessary to her."[35] In Cambodia, Laos, and Vietnam, France gave itself leeway in its planned withdrawal so that it could keep some troops in place, if the host country agreed. "The Government of the

33 Peace Treaty Between Israel and Egypt, 1979, Appendix to Annex I.

34 Agreement on the Conclusions of the Internationalist Mission of the Cuban Military Contingent, 1988, Art. 3.

35 Évian Accords, 1962, Ch. III.

French Republic declares that it is ready to withdraw its troops from the territory of Cambodia, Laos and Viet-Nam, at the request of the Governments concerned and within a period which shall be fixed by agreement between the parties, except in the cases where, by agreement between the two parties, a certain number of French troops shall remain at specified points and for a specified time."[36]

In the case of the Allied withdrawal from Japan, the agreement made clear that the Allied countries retained the option to maintain military bases in Japan. "Nothing in this provision shall . . . prevent the stationing or retention of foreign armed forces in Japanese territory under or in consequence of any bilateral or multilateral agreements which have been or may be made between one or more of the Allied Powers, on the one hand, and Japan on the other."[37] The two agreements signed by Iraq and the United States in 2008, the Strategic Framework Agreement and the Status of Forces Agreement, by contrast, explicitly placed limitations on the future presence of the U.S. troops. First, the Strategic Framework Agreement acknowledges that "the temporary presence of U.S. forces in Iraq is at the request and invitation of the sovereign Government of Iraq and with full respect for the sovereignty of Iraq." More to the point, the parties agreed that "the United States shall not . . . seek or request permanent bases or a permanent military presence in Iraq."[38] Second, the Status of Forces Agreement provides detailed guidelines for what U.S. troops can and cannot do and where they can and cannot operate in the time between the signing of the agreement and the scheduled withdrawal.[39]

---

36 Final Declaration of the Geneva Conference on the Problem of Restoring Peace in Indo-China, Geneva, Switzerland, July 21, 1954, Art. 10, "Declaration by the Government of the French Republic."

37 Treaty of Peace with Japan, 1951, Ch. III, Art. 6 (a).

38 United States of America and the Republic of Iraq, Strategic Framework Agreement for a Relationship of Friendship and Cooperation, Baghdad, Iraq, November 17, 2008b, Sec. I, paras. 3 and 4.

39 U.S.–Iraq Status of Forces Agreement, 2008a, passim.

Withdrawal of Foreign Troops: Cases of Civil Wars

The agreements that end civil wars that do not involve major-power intervention differ from the agreements just discussed in several ways, two of which merit brief discussion. First, several of the negotiated settlements to civil wars present a conditional timeline for withdrawal. The cases of decolonization and military occupations, by contrast, generally have unconditional withdrawals. The civil war agreements condition withdrawal either on domestic benchmarks or the deployment of international forces. In Mozambique's Rome Accords, for example, withdrawal is conditioned on domestic processes: "The withdrawal of foreign troops from Mozambican territory shall be initiated following the entry into force of the cease-fire (E-Day)," which is the day the legislature adopts the agreement and enters it into law.[40] The actions of international bodies set the pace of foreign troop withdrawal in Sierra Leone, Guinea-Bissau, and Rwanda. In Sierra Leone's Abidjan Accords, withdrawal was to be "no later than three months after the deployment of the Neutral Monitoring Group or six months after the signing of the Peace Agreement, whichever is earlier."[41] In Guinea-Bissau's Abuja Agreement, "This withdrawal shall be done simultaneously with the deployment of an ECOWAS [Economic Community of West African States] Military Observer Group interposition force, which will take over from the withdrawn forces."[42] And in Rwanda's N'sele Ceasefire

[40] Republic of Mozambique and RENAMO, General Peace Agreement for Mozambique ("Rome Accords"), Rome, Italy, October 4, 1992, Protocol IV, Art. II, Sec. 1.

[41] Government of Sierra Leone and the Revolutionary United Front of Sierra Leone, Peace Agreement between the Government of the Republic of Sierra Leone and the Revolutionary United Front of Sierra Leone ("Abidjan Accords"), Abidjan, Côte d'Ivoire, November 30, 1996, Art. 12. Regarding the Neutral Monitoring Group mentioned in this quotation, Art. 11 states, "A Neutral Monitoring Group (NMG) from the international community shall be responsible for monitoring breaches of the ceasefire provided under this Peace Agreement. Both Parties upon signing this Agreement shall request the international community to provide neutral monitors. Such monitors when deployed shall be in position for an initial period of three months."

[42] Government of Guinea-Bissau and the Self-Proclaimed Military Junta, Agreement Between the Government of Guinea-Bissau and the Self-Proclaimed Military Junta ("Abuja Peace Agreement"), Abuja, Nigeria, November 1, 1998, para. 2.

Agreement, "The withdrawal of all foreign troops [would occur] after the effective deployment of the Neutral Military Observer Group."[43]

Second, some of the civil war agreements contain provisions for monitoring and verification of foreign withdrawal that are not seen in the major global or regional power cases. Unlike the issue of conditional withdrawal, which seems plausibly suitable to conflicts involving major-power intervention, the monitoring and verification processes established in these agreements are not something that a major power, and especially the United States, would likely agree to. This is because these provisions give significant control over foreign troops to the United Nations. In Angola, there was to be a "handover to the UN of members of foreign military forces . . . for purposes of repatriation of personnel to their countries of origin."[44] And Cambodia's Paris Agreement gave the United Nations Transitional Authority in Cambodia (UNTAC) the authority and mandate to "supervise, monitor and verify the withdrawal . . . of all categories of foreign forces, advisers and military personnel and their weapons, ammunition and equipment, and their non-return to Cambodia."[45] To fulfill its mission, each foreign party had to provide UNTAC with "detailed information in writing regarding the withdrawal of foreign forces," including "[t]otal strength of these forces and their organization and deployment; [c]omprehensive lists of arms, ammunition and equipment held by these forces, and their exact locations; [and] [w]ithdrawal plan (already implemented or to be implemented), including withdrawal routes, border crossing points and time of departure from Cambodia." Then UNTAC also was authorized to "immediately deploy military personnel with the foreign forces and accompany them until they have withdrawn from Cambodian territory. UNTAC will also establish checkpoints on with-

---

43 Government of the Republic of Rwanda and the Rwandese Patriotic Front, N'sele Ceasefire Agreement, Arusha, Tanzania, July 22, 1992, Art. II, Sec. 6

44 Government of the Republic of Angola and the National Union for the Total Independence of Angola (UNITA), Memorandum of Understanding ("Luena Agreement"), Luena, Angola, April 4, 2002, Annex I/A, Sec. 1.2 (f).

45 Agreement on a Comprehensive Political Settlement of the Cambodia Conflict ("Paris Peace Agreements"), Paris, France, October 23, 1991, Annex I, Sec. C, paras. 1 and 1(a).

drawal routes, border crossing points and airfields to verify the withdrawal and ensure the non-return of all categories of foreign forces."[46]

Political Power-Sharing

The term *power-sharing* poses a conundrum for peacemaking in Afghanistan. Although the concepts of political inclusion of relevant groups and the distribution of power among them are clearly central to the actual practice of Afghan politics, power-sharing has a negative connotation in Afghan political discourse. Two factors further complicate discussions of power-sharing solutions. First, there is uncertainty among the parties about whether power-sharing is acceptable to all the stakeholders: Would non-Taliban stakeholders accept the Taliban into government, and would the Taliban be willing to join a coalition government with other stakeholders? The 2016 power-sharing agreement reached between the Afghan government and Gulbuddin Hekmatyar suggests that Afghan elites might be willing to accept a role for the Taliban in government in principle, but the details will matter greatly. Although the Taliban's leadership states that it is not seeking a monopoly on power, it is unclear as yet whether the Taliban rank and file share that view.[47] Thus, neither party can entirely trust the commitments made by the other.

The second complication is that power-sharing is a broad and often ill-defined idea that encompasses a wide range of political arrangements. Thus, discussions of the subject are frequently confused, and parties hold varying interpretations and preconceptions of the idea. The general dislike of power-sharing in Afghanistan is primarily due to a dislike of forced coalition government and territorial division of the country, but there are formulas that could get around these objections.

Despite these difficulties, it seems likely that any settlement to end the fighting in Afghanistan must centrally feature power-sharing, by which we mean "formal institutions that distribute decisionmaking

[46] Paris Peace Agreements, 1991, Annex 2, Art. VI, Secs. 1 and 3.

[47] Osman and Gopal, 2016, pp. 12–16.

rights within the state and define decisionmaking procedures."[48] Scholars have identified power-sharing institutions across four dimensions of power: political, military, territorial, and economic.[49] Our discussion here is limited to political power-sharing, the most prevalent form, though we discuss military power-sharing in a later section.[50]

Although critics and skeptics of power-sharing remain, there are by now several decades of research showing that power-sharing increases the likelihood of peace and stability in plural and postconflict societies.[51] Proponents of power-sharing argue that these institutions ensure that all the parties know that their interests—including their survival—will be protected after the war. "By dividing and balancing power among rival groups," write political scientists Caroline Hartzell and Matthew Hoddie, "power-sharing institutions minimize the danger of any one party becoming dominant and threatening the security of others."[52] Critics, however, argue that, especially in the absence of third-party

---

48 Donald Rothchild and Philip G. Roeder, "Power Sharing as an Impediment to Peace and Democracy," in Philip G. Roeder and Donald Rothchild, eds., *Sustainable Peace: Power and Democracy After Civil Wars*, Ithaca, N.Y.: Cornell University Press, 2005, p. 30. Hartzell and Hoddie's widely used definition of "power-sharing institutions" is "rules that, in addition to defining how decisions will be made by groups within the polity, allocate decision-making rights, including access to state resources, among collectivities competing for power"; Hartzell and Hoddie, 2003, p. 320.

49 Hartzell and Hoddie, 2003, p. 320; Caroline A. Hartzell and Matthew Hoddie, "The Art of the Possible: Power Sharing and Post–Civil War Democracy," *World Politics*, Vol. 67, No. 1, January 2015, pp. 40–43; Mattes and Savun, 2009.

50 Mattes and Savun, 2009, p. 749.

51 For example, Arend Lijphart, *Democracy in Plural Societies: A Comparative Exploration*, New Haven, Conn.: Yale University Press, 1977; Donald L. Horowitz, *Ethnic Groups in Conflict*, Berkeley, Calif.: University of California Press, 1985; Hartzell and Hoddie, 2003; Caroline A. Hartzell and Matthew Hoddie, *Crafting Peace: Power-Sharing Institutions and the Negotiated Settlement of Civil Wars*, University Park, Pa.: Penn State University Press, 2007; Lars-Erik Cederman, Andreas Wimmer, and Brian Min, "Why Do Ethnic Groups Rebel?: New Data and Analysis," *World Politics*, Vol. 62, No. 1, January 2010; Melani Cammett and Edmund Malesky, "Power Sharing in Postconflict Societies: Implications for Peace and Governance," *Journal of Conflict Resolution*, Vol. 56, No. 6, 2012; Hartzell and Hoddie, 2015; and Philip Roessler and David Ohls, "Self-Enforcing Power Sharing in Weak States," *International Organization*, Vol. 72, No. 2, Spring 2018.

52 Hartzell and Hoddie, 2003, p. 319.

guarantors, these commitments to share power peacefully are not credible and that such institutions contain the seeds of their own long-term destruction.[53] Although power-sharing cannot be embraced unthinkingly, the evidence suggests that it is still better to have power-sharing in an agreement than to not. And given the stalemate in the Afghan conflict, with no party able to militarily defeat the other, there are no plausible solutions besides power-sharing institutions.

The rest of this section reviews options for power-sharing arrangements that have been tried in recent comprehensive peace agreements.

Who Shares Power?

A primary decision that must be made in any power-sharing arrangement is who the power-sharing parties are. In other words, how are the power-sharing stakeholders defined? Past agreements define the power-sharing partners in one of two ways: socially or organizationally. Social group–based power-sharing makes guarantees of representation to social groups, generally ethnic groups but sometimes groups defined by another characteristic, such as residents of a particular territory. Organization-based power-sharing, by contrast, makes guarantees to specific organizations, generally rebel groups or opposition political parties.

Many of the marquee power-sharing agreements of recent decades are examples of ethnic power-sharing: the Taif Accords in Lebanon, Dayton Agreement in Bosnia-Herzegovina (hereafter "Bosnia"), and Good Friday Agreement in Northern Ireland. In these cases, political inclusion is secured for ethnic groups involved in the conflict, not the specific organizations that represent them. This way, the ethnic groups have the ability to select their own representatives. The Taif Accords, for instance, establishes seats in the Lebanese parliament for "Christians and Muslims . . . [and] the denominations of each sect."[54] Likewise, the Good Friday Agreement sets up power-sharing

---

[53] Barbara F. Walter, *Committing to Peace: The Successful Settlement of Civil Wars*, Princeton, N.J.: Princeton University Press, 2002; Rothchild and Roeder, 2005.

[54] Document of National Accord ("Taif Accords"), Taif, Saudi Arabia, October 22, 1989, Art. II, Sec. A.5.

between "unionists" and "nationalists," and the Dayton Agreement does the same for Croats, Bosniacs, and Serbs.[55] But social groups that are party to a peace agreement need not be ethnically defined. The Mindanao Final Agreement in the Philippines, which ended a conflict over regional autonomy, included provisions to ensure that Mindanao island had representation in the national government. For instance, the agreement requires the national Cabinet to include at least one department secretary "who is an inhabitant of the Autonomous Region to be recommended by the Head of the Autonomous Government."[56]

Rather than establish power-sharing institutions for social groups, some agreements make guarantees to specific organizations. Sierra Leone's Lomé Agreement set up power-sharing between the government and the Revolutionary United Front (RUF) rebel group.[57] Guinea-Bissau's Abuja Peace Agreement stated that the postwar government would include "representatives of the self-proclaimed junta."[58] Liberia's Accra Accord divvied up seats in the transitional legislature to the government and two rebel groups, as well as "Political Parties," "Civil Society and Special Interest Groups," and the "Counties."[59] Tajikistan's settlement guaranteed the incorporation of "representatives of the United Tajik Opposition into the structures of the executive

55 Good Friday Agreement, 1998, Strand 1, paras. 5(d) and 6; Dayton Agreement, 1995, e.g., Annex 4, Art. IV.

56 Government of the Republic of the Philippines and the Moro National Liberation Front, The Final Agreement on the Implementation of the 1976 Tripoli Agreement Between the Government of the Republic of the Philippines and the Moro National Liberation Front ("Mindanao Final Agreement"), Manila, Philippines, September 2, 1996, Art. 65.

57 Government of Sierra Leone and the Revolutionary United Front of Sierra Leone, Peace Agreement Between the Government of Sierra Leone and the Revolutionary United Front of Sierra Leone ("Lomé Peace Agreement"), Lomé, Togo, July 7, 1999, Art. V.

58 Abuja Peace Agreement, 1998, para. 4.

59 Government of the Republic of Liberia, Liberians United for Reconciliation and Democracy, and Movement for Democracy in Liberia, Accra Comprehensive Peace Agreement, Accra, Ghana, August 18, 2003, Art. XXIV, para. 4.

branch."[60] Rwanda's Arusha Accords gives seats in the government to six named parties.[61]

It is also possible to combine the two pathways to representation in one agreement. Burundi's Arusha Accords uses both social group and party-based power-sharing. Social group–based power-sharing ensures that the Senate has "three individuals from the Twa ethnic group" and "respect for the political, regional and ethnic balances." At the same time, organization-based power-sharing gives the main rebel group guaranteed positions in the government.[62]

How to Share Power?

There are two main forms of power-sharing arrangements found in the agreements we examined: *mandates* and *opportunities*. Mandates, as identified by political scientists Donald Rothchild and Philip Roeder, are "relatively hard guarantees of representation in decisionmaking [that] stipulate that specific ethnic groups must occupy designated posts of the central government." Opportunities are "relatively soft guarantees" of "representation in central decisionmaking . . . [that] do not assign government posts to specific ethnic groups but provide selection procedures that increase the probability that all major ethnic groups will in fact be represented."[63] Although these definitions are written specifically to apply to ethnic groups, the logic of mandates and opportunities applies to any social group or political organization.

---

60 Government of Tajikistan and United Tajik Opposition, Protocol on Political Questions, Bishkek, Kyrgyzstan, May 18, 1997a, Art. 3.

61 Government of the Republic of Rwanda and the Rwandese Patriotic Front, Peace Agreement Between the Government of the Republic of Rwanda and the Rwandese Patriotic Front ("Rwandan Arusha Accords"), Arusha, Tanzania, August 4, 1993b, Ch. VII, Sec. 1, Subsec. 4.

62 Government of Burundi et al., Arusha Peace and Reconciliation Agreement for Burundi ("Burundian Arusha Accords"), Arusha, Tanzania, August 28, 2000, Protocol II, Ch. II, Art. 15.

63 Rothchild and Roeder, 2005, pp. 31–32; also, Cammett and Malesky, 2012, p. 985.

Mandated Power-Sharing

In the agreements we studied, two mechanisms to mandate power-sharing are implemented: quotas and assignments. Both forms of mandates can be used to share power among either social groups or specific organizations.

Quotas. Quotas specify either the number or proportion of seats in the cabinet or legislature for a relevant group. Mandated quotas for social groups were established in several agreements. In Lebanon, for example, the Taif Accords stated, "the parliamentary seats shall be divided according to the following bases: a. Equally between Christians and Muslims. b. Proportionately between the denominations of each sect. c. Proportionately between the districts."[64] In Bosnia, the Dayton Agreement established as a chamber of its legislature a House of Peoples with 15 members, five from each ethnic group. The rules of quorum require that at least three representatives of each group be present to conduct business. Additionally, the Dayton Agreement created a three-person presidency, requiring there to be one Bosniac, one Croat, and one Serb.[65] And in the Mindanao Final Agreement, the Philippines agreed to bring representatives from Mindanao into various positions across the government. For example, the parties agreed that at least one Cabinet member must be an inhabitant of Mindanao, and "at least one official in each of the departments and the constitutional bodies of the national government" must come from the island as well.[66]

Quotas can be used to guarantee the representation of political parties or armed groups. Agreements such as the ones reached in Liberia, Sudan, and Tajikistan used this method of power-sharing. In Liberia, numerous parties and armed groups were assigned a set number of seats in the National Transitional Legislative Assembly.[67] Sudan's 2005 Comprehensive Peace Agreement stipulated that the "cabinet

---

64 Taif Accords, 1989, Art. II, Sec. A.5.

65 Dayton Agreement, 1995, Annex 4, Art. IV, Sec. 9, and Annex 4, Art. 5.

66 Mindanao Final Agreement, 1996, Arts. 65 and 66.

67 Accra Comprehensive Peace Agreement, 2003, Art. XXIV, Sec. 4.

posts and portfolios" in Sudan's government "shall be shared equitably and qualitatively by the two Parties." Additionally, the agreement distributed a set percentage of the "seats of the National Executive" to the relevant parties.[68] And in Tajikistan, "[t]he reform of the Government shall be carried out by incorporating representatives of the United Tajik Opposition [UTO] into the structures of the executive branch, including ministries, departments, local government bodies and judicial and law-enforcement bodies on the basis of a quota."[69] Furthermore, there was to be a "Commission on National Reconciliation with equal representation of the Parties and headed by a representative of UTO" and a requirement "to reserve for representatives of the Opposition (UTO) thirty percent of posts in the executive power structures and twenty-five percent of seats in the Central Electoral Commission."[70]

Assignments. Rather than give social groups or organizations quotas, several agreements assigned specific government positions to named parties or individuals. In Angola, for instance, specific ministries, governorships, and even ambassadorships were assigned to UNITA, the main rebel group.[71] In Sierra Leone, Foday Sankoh, the leader of the RUF rebel group, was named board chair of the Commission for the Management of Strategic Resources, National Reconstruction, and Development. "For this purpose," the agreement stated, "he shall enjoy the status of Vice President and shall therefore be answerable only to the President of Sierra Leone."[72]

---

68 Government of the Republic of the Sudan and Sudan People's Liberation Movement/ Sudan People's Liberation Army, The Comprehensive Peace Agreement, Naivasha, Kenya, January 9, 2005, Ch. II, Part II, Sec. 2.5, paras. 3 and 5.

69 Protocol on Political Questions, 1997a, Art. 3.

70 Government of Tajikistan and United Tajik Opposition, Protocol on the Guarantees of Implementation of the General Agreement on Establishment of Peace and National Accord in Tajikistan, Tehran, Iran, May 28, 1997b, Art. 1.

71 Government of the Republic of Angola and the National Union for the Total Independence of Angola (UNITA), Lusaka Protocol, Lusaka, Zambia, November 15, 1994, "Document Relating to UNITA's Participation in the Central, Provincial and Local Administration and in the Diplomatic Missions Abroad, in Accordance with Art. I of the Modalities of National Reconciliation."

72 Lomé Peace Agreement, 1999, Art. V, para. 2.

However, the Lomé Agreement also illustrates a more flexible option for portioning out government positions that sits between a quota and an assignment: The rebel group was guaranteed at least one senior government position, but the exact position was not agreed on in the text. Specifically, in addition to Sankoh's assignment, the RUF was offered "one of the senior cabinet appointments such as finance, foreign affairs and justice," in addition to a quota of three other cabinet posts and four deputy minister positions.[73]

Opportunity-Based Power-Sharing

Opportunity-based power-sharing is less common than mandated power-sharing in the agreements examined. Power-sharing opportunities come in two flavors: opportunities in the rules of representation and opportunities in the rules of decisionmaking. Rules of representation can foster power-sharing by increasing the number of groups represented in government. Rules of decisionmaking can foster power-sharing by requiring diversity and inclusiveness in the making of important decisions.

Rules that augment diverse representation in government are found, for instance, in the agreements reached in South Africa, Burundi, and Northern Ireland.[74] In South Africa, "[e]very party holding at least 80 seats in the National Assembly shall be entitled to designate an Executive Deputy President from among the members of the National Assembly."[75] This ensures that all sizable parties have representation at a senior level. In Burundi, two clauses ensure diversity at the highest level of the executive: "The President and the Vice-President of the transitional National Assembly shall come from two different political families" and "The first transitional President and Vice-President of the Republic shall come from different ethnic groups

---

73 Lomé Peace Agreement, 1999, Art. V, paras. 3–4.

74 One common recommendation for increasing the representativeness of government is to establish a parliamentary system rather than a presidential system. Several agreements do so, but we focus in this section on mechanisms that are more explicitly tailored to power-sharing.

75 Republic of South Africa, Constitution of 1993 ("Interim Constitution"), Act No. 200 of 1993, January 24, 1994, Ch. 4, Sec. 84, para. 1.

and political parties."[76] And Northern Ireland uses representation rules for committee assignments ("allocations of Committee Chairs, Ministers and Committee membership in proportion to party strengths").[77]

Burundi and Northern Ireland are also examples of cases that used the rules of decisionmaking to encourage power-sharing. In Burundi, the Arusha Accords required a supermajority of two-thirds of the transitional legislature to pass legislation.[78] Northern Ireland's Good Friday Agreement created several "safeguards to ensure that all sections of the community can participate and work together successfully in the operation of these institutions and that all sections of the community are protected."[79] Multiple mechanisms that foster inclusive decisionmaking were established, but the most important are the two "arrangements to ensure key decisions are taken on a cross-community basis": "parallel consent" and "a weighed majority." When an issue is determined to be of vital interest to one or both ethnic communities, legislation can only be passed if the requirements of one of the two mechanisms are met.[80] Parallel consent means that the bill must receive support from "a majority of those members present and voting, including a majority of the unionist and nationalist designations present and voting." Weighted majority means that the bill must receive support from a 60-percent supermajority "of members present and voting, including at least 40% of each of the nationalist and unionist designations present and voting."[81]

---

76 Burundian Arusha Accords, 2000, Protocol II, Ch. II, Art. 15, Secs. 8(b) and 12.

77 Good Friday Agreement, 1998, Strand 1, para. 5(a).

78 Burundian Arusha Accords, 2000, Protocol II, Ch. II, Art. 15, Sec. 10.

79 Good Friday Agreement, 1998, Strand 1, para. 5.

80 The mechanisms for designating an issue for this process are themselves rules that foster inclusive decisionmaking. Some "decisions requiring cross-community support will be designated in advance, including election of the Chair of the Assembly, the First Minister and Deputy First Minister, standing orders and budget allocations." But the mechanisms can also "be triggered by a petition of concern brought by a significant minority of Assembly members (30/108)." Good Friday Agreement, 1998, Strand 1, para. 5(d)(ii).

81 Good Friday Agreement, 1998, Strand 1, paras. 5(d) (i)–(ii).

The academic literature provides additional suggestions for designing institutions that increase opportunities for power-sharing that were not included in the agreements reviewed for this research. For instance, several scholars recommend voting systems that are not winner-take-all, a problematic feature of first-past-the-post single-member districts. Methods to avoid this pitfall include proportional representation and multimember districts. As Rothchild and Roeder argue, "constitutional designers can increase the likelihood of coalition governments that over time include most of the major ethnic groups by adopting a combination of parliamentary government with elections by list proportional representation in large-magnitude districts with low electoral thresholds."[82]

Transitional Power-Sharing Versus Permanent Power-Sharing

A third question about power sharing that agreements must address is whether the arrangement is temporary or permanent. Examples of both interim power-sharing governments and permanent power-sharing institutions are found in the agreements we reviewed. The temporary arrangements often take the form of mandated power-sharing transitional governments. In fact, political scientist Nina Caspersen observes that "in non-territorial conflicts, the use of transitional power-sharing arrangements has emerged as the dominant model."[83] Such mandates can set quotas for the postwar transitional executive and/or legislature, or they can assign positions to specific individuals. Liberia's National Transitional Legislative Assembly, for example, featured seats assigned to various parties.[84] Sudan's Comprehensive Peace Agreement created mandated quotas for the interim executive that was to govern "prior to elections," at which point the newly elected government would assume power.[85] The Taif Accords is an example of a notionally temporary arrangement that appears to be permanent. The agreement notes Lebanon's aspiration for a postsectarian political system, at which point

[82] Rothchild and Roeder, 2005, p. 32.

[83] Caspersen, 2017, p. 126.

[84] Accra Comprehensive Peace Agreement, 2003, Art. XXIV, Sec. 4.

[85] Comprehensive Peace Agreement (Sudan), 2005, Ch. II, Part II, Sec. 2.5, para. 5.

the confessional quotas could disappear. As the agreement stipulates, the mandated proportionality should only exist "until the Chamber of Deputies passes an election law free of sectarian restriction"—a step that has not yet been taken.[86]

Permanent power-sharing structures can take the form of mandates or opportunities. In either case, they establish governance institutions that are intended to last and are not restricted to a transitional period. For instance, the Dayton Agreement established permanent ethnic quotas in Bosnia's government, while the Good Friday Agreement created permanent institutions in Northern Ireland with elements of opportunity-based and mandated power-sharing.[87]

Security Power-Sharing

Security concerns tend to be acute in the aftermath of violent conflict. As a result, a central task of a peace settlement is to ameliorate those concerns. A commonly attempted solution in peace agreements has been to formally share power in security institutions, an arrangement, generally called *military power-sharing*, that "seeks to distribute authority within the coercive apparatus of the state."[88] Roughly 60 percent of negotiated settlements reached in civil wars between 1945 and 2005 contained some form of military power-sharing.[89] There are three typical ways of achieving this objective. First, the warring armed forces can be integrated into a "unified state security force."[90] Such integration can maintain military units "constituted on the basis of their members' communal, organizational, or ideological affiliation"

---

[86] Taif Accords, 1989, Art. II, Sec. A, para. 5.

[87] Dayton Agreement, 1995, Annex 4, Arts. IV–V; and Good Friday Agreement, 1998, Strand 1.

[88] Hartzell and Hoddie, 2015, p. 42.

[89] Mattes and Savun, 2009, p. 749. Caroline Hartzell, using a more expansive definition of civil war settlement, finds that less than 40 percent contained military integration provisions; Caroline A. Hartzell, "Mixed Motives? Explaining the Decision to Integrate Militaries at Civil War's End," in Roy Licklider, ed., *New Armies from Old: Merging Competing Military Forces After Civil Wars*, Washington, D.C.: Georgetown University Press, 2014, p. 13.

[90] Hartzell and Hoddie, 2015, p. 42. Also, Mattes and Savun, 2009, p. 749.

(low horizontal integration) or integrate at the unit level by assigning troops to units without consideration of their affiliation (high horizontal integration).[91] Second, representatives of all the warring parties can be appointed to leadership positions in the state's security forces, integrating the officer corps (vertical integration).[92] Third, and least commonly, a deal can be struck to allow the warring parties to maintain their own armed forces.[93]

Whether integrating Taliban and Afghan government forces (both rank and file and officers) will be acceptable on leadership and individual levels and be practically feasible is uncertain. After all, such integration would involve bringing together people who have spent much of their lives at war with each other and who have little reason to trust one another. These concerns, however, are not unique to Afghanistan and plague many, if not all, post–civil war societies contemplating military power-sharing.[94]

Integration of Forces

Creating new security forces composed of former insurgent and government troops is the most straightforward path toward military integration. The primary distinction among approaches to the merger of forces that emerged from our review of peace agreements was whether or not integration is predicated on a stated principle of inclusion. Several agreements feature an explicit goal of representativeness in the armed forces toward which integration is to contribute. For example,

---

91 Ronald R. Krebs and Roy Licklider, "United They Fall: Why the International Community Should Not Promote Military Integration After Civil War," *International Security*, Vol. 40, No. 3, Winter 2015/2016, p. 100.

92 Hartzell and Hoddie, 2015, p. 42; Mattes and Savun, 2009, p. 749; Krebs and Licklider, 2015/2016, p. 101.

93 Hartzell and Hoddie, 2015, p. 42.

94 In many cases, the skepticism appears to be well-founded. A recent analysis by Krebs and Licklider concludes that military integration, particularly when it is pushed by the international community without local demand, can lead to more harm than good. Krebs and Licklider are less skeptical of "military integration when it emerges organically from negotiations among local combatants," but even then find it to be risky and far from a panacea; Krebs and Licklider, 2015/2016, quotation is from p. 96.

Liberia's Accra Agreement states, "The restructured [security] force shall take into account the country's national balance. It shall be composed without any political bias to ensure that it represents the national character of Liberia."[95] Mali's 2015 agreement commits to "[i]nclusivity and substantial representation of all the populations of Mali within the armed and security forces."[96] At the most extreme end, an agreement can specify a quota to ensure representation of a social or armed group. For instance, both Angola's Lusaka Protocol and Mozambique's General Peace Agreement require that the state security forces have equal numbers of government and rebel troops.[97] Many other agreements, however, propose integrating forces without articulating the principle behind the merger, which can leave open the question of what constitutes successful achievement of the goal. In the 2009 agreement between the Democratic Republic of Congo and the National Congress for the Defense of the People (CNDP), to take one example, the CNDP committed "to integrate its police and armed unit elements respectively in the Congolese National Police Force and the Armed Forces of the Democratic Republic of Congo."[98] But the agreement adds no detail on the expected composition of the integrated security forces.

Vertical Integration

In seeking to reassure members of a population that their security interests will be protected by the state's security services, it can be insufficient to merely integrate the rank and file. Integrating the higher echelon leadership roles is also important. Several of the agreements

---

95 Accra Comprehensive Peace Agreement, 2003, Art. VII, Sec. 2 (b).

96 Government of the Republic of Mali et al., Agreement for Peace and Reconciliation in Mali Resulting from the Algiers Process, Bamako, Mali, May 15, 2015, Sec. III, Ch. 7, Art. 17.

97 Lusaka Protocol, 1994, Annex 4, Sec. III; Rome Accords, 1992, Protocol IV, Art. I, Sec. ii, para. 2. In Angola, the "principle of parity" only applied to the army. The navy and the air force had different rules.

98 Government of the Democratic Republic of the Congo and the Congrès National pour la Défense du Peuple (CNDP), Peace Agreement, Goma, Democratic Republic of Congo, March 23, 2009, Art. 1, Sec. 1.1 (a)

reviewed incorporate balance in the officer corps as a part of military integration. Burundi's Arusha Accords states that "[c]ommand posts shall be distributed on the basis of competence and merit while ensuring the necessary ethnic balances." In order to rectify the "command-level imbalances," the agreement further commits to "accelerated training of commissioned and non-commissioned officers from among the combatants of the political parties and movements."[99] Furthermore, Burundi's postconflict constitution of 2005 stipulates that "the Minister in charge of National Defense is not from the same ethnic group as the Minister responsible for the National Police."[100] In the Democratic Republic of Congo, the government agreed to "formally recognise the ranks of ex-CNDP elements in both the Congolese National Police and [armed forces]."[101]

Joint Commissions

A common mechanism for ensuring that the parties follow through on their military power-sharing commitments is to establish a joint commission. The joint commission itself is also a form of power-sharing because it brings representatives of the former warring parties together in a decisionmaking or consultative body. Although the joint commissions differ from one another in certain aspects (in the scope of their mandate and the composition of membership, for instance), they are fairly similar across the agreements examined. Overall, they entail bringing together representatives from the agreements' signatories to monitor the integration of troops and/or the ceasefire. Angola's Lusaka Protocol, for example, set up a working group composed of representatives of the government, UNITA, and the United Nations that is "responsible for monitoring . . . tasks concerning the completion of

---

[99] Burundian Arusha Accords, 2000, Protocol III, Ch. II, Arts. 13.4 and 16.4

[100] Republic of Burundi, Constitution, March 18, 2005, Title V, Art. 130. The Arusha Accords has a similar clause for Burundi's transitional government. See Burundian Arusha Accords, 2000, Protocol II, Ch. II, Art. 15, Sec. 15 (b).

[101] Peace Agreement (Government of the Democratic Republic of the Congo and CNDP), 2009, Art 12, Sec. 12.8.

the formation of [the armed forces] and demobilization."[102] And Bosnia's Dayton Agreement established a Joint Military Commission to

> (a) Serve as the central body for all Parties to this Annex to bring any military complaints, questions, or problems that require resolution by the IFOR Commander, such as allegations of cease-fire violations or other noncompliance with this Annex. (b) Receive reports and agree on specific actions to ensure compliance with the provisions of this Annex by the Parties. (c) Assist the IFOR Commander in determining and implementing a series of local transparency measures between the Parties.[103]

Kosovo's proposed Rambouillet Agreement had a very similar joint commission mandate.[104]

There is some variation among joint commissions having to do with the presence of international parties and decisionmaking rules. International parties were made members of the joint commissions for Angola's Lusaka Protocol ("representatives of the United Nations"), Mozambique ("representatives of the countries selected by the Parties to advise in the process"), Bosnia ("chaired by the IFOR Commander"), and Mali (chaired by a representative of the United Nations Multidimensional Integrated Stabilization Mission in Mali).[105] By contrast, the joint commission established by Angola's Cabinda agreement and South Sudan's 2015 agreement only included domestic parties.[106] The introduction of international members to a joint commission opens up

---

[102] Lusaka Protocol, 1994, Annex 4, Sec. III.

[103] Dayton Agreement, 1995, Annex 1-A, Art. VIII, Sec. 2.

[104] Interim Agreement for Peace and Self-Government in Kosovo ("Rambouillet Agreement"), Rambouillet, France, February 23, 1999, Ch. 7, Art. XI, Sec. 2.

[105] Lusaka Protocol, 1994, Annex 4, Sec. III; Rome Accords, 1992, Protocol V, Art. I, Sec. iii, para. 1; Dayton Agreement, 1995, Annex 1-A, Art. VIII, Sec. 3; Agreement for Peace and Reconciliation in Mali Resulting from the Algiers Process, 2015, Annex 2, Sec. I (a).

[106] Government of the Republic of Angola and the Cabinda Forum for Dialogue, Memorandum of Understanding for Peace and Reconciliation of the Province of Cabinda, Namibe, Angola, August 1, 2006, Ch. III, Art. A, Sec. 1 (a); Republic of South Sudan and Sudan People's Liberation Movement-in-Opposition, Agreement on the Resolution of the Conflict in the Republic of South Sudan, Addis Ababa, Ethiopia, August 17, 2015, Sec. II, Sec. 3.3.

new methods for decisionmaking in the commission and for neutral interpretation of implementation requirements. For instance, Angola's Cabinda agreement's exclusively domestic joint commission alternates its chairmanship between government and opposition representatives and makes all decisions by consensus.[107] Bosnia and Kosovo, on the other hand, whose commissions had international chairs, gave ultimate decisionmaking powers to the foreign representatives. As the Dayton Agreement states, "To the extent possible, problems shall be solved promptly by mutual agreement. However, all final decisions concerning its military matters shall be made by the IFOR Commander."[108]

International Roles

In addition to the option of including international parties in a joint commission, peace agreements carve out other international roles in their security institution power-sharing mechanisms. At the extreme end, international peacekeeping missions were essentially in charge of security issues in such places as Bosnia and Kosovo. In other cases, international actors played lesser but still important roles. For instance, in Angola's Lusaka Protocol, the United Nations was designated to receive information on "the personnel, the composition and location of the respective military forces" so that the joint commission could carry out its missions.[109] Liberia's Accra Agreement requested several multilateral bodies to assist with its "security reform effort" and singled out the United States to "play a lead role in organising this [military] restructuring program."[110] And Macedonia's Ohrid Agreement

---

The Cabinda agreement includes domestic religious institutions in addition to political institutions.

[107] Government of the Republic of Angola and the Cabinda Forum for Dialogue, 2006, Ch. III, Art. A, Sec. 1 (c).

[108] Dayton Agreement, 1995, Annex 1-A, Art. VIII, Sec. 5.

[109] Lusaka Protocol, 1994, Annex 4, Sec. III.

[110] Accra Comprehensive Peace Agreement, 2003, Art. VII, Sec. 1 (b).

"invite[d] the international community to support and assist with the implementation of these [security power-sharing] commitments."[111]

Constitutional Reform

One of the Taliban's major demands for a peace agreement is a new or revised constitution because they were excluded from the process that developed Afghanistan's 2004 Constitution. Adopting a new constitution or significantly amending an existing constitution is a common feature of peace agreements. According to the coding of the PAM database, 19 out of 34 comprehensive peace agreements reached between 1989 and 2012 included constitutional reform provisions (56 percent).[112] A separate analysis by Christine Bell and Kimana Zulueta-Füscher finds 23 cases of political settlement processes that produced a "final" constitution.[113] They find, however, that the cases did not all follow the same path toward a constitution. They classify four distinct sequences that end in a new or fundamentally revised constitution in the aftermath of violence: (1) a peace agreement that leads directly to a new or revised constitution, (2) a peace agreement with transitional political arrangements that lead to a new or revised constitution, (3) an interim constitution that serves as a peace agreement and then leads to a new constitution, and (4) a peace agreement with transitional political arrangements that lead to an interim constitution, which is superseded by a final constitution.[114] Their conclusion is that the sequencing is important and "peace mediators and constitutional advisors must pay attention" to it, but there is no single model appropriate for every country. Rather, finding a suitable order of events

---

[111] Republic of Macedonia, Internal Macedonian Revolutionary Organization – Democratic Party for Macedonian National Unit, Democratic Party of Albanians, Social Democratic Union of Macedonia, and Party for Democratic Prosperity, Framework Agreement ("Ohrid Agreement"), Ohrid, Macedonia, August 13, 2001, Annex C, Art. 5.2.

[112] Joshi, Quinn, and Regan, 2015, p. 556.

[113] Christine Bell and Kimana Zulueta-Fülscher, *Sequencing Peace Agreements and Constitutions in the Political Settlement Process*, Stockholm, Sweden: International IDEA, November 2016, p. 21.

[114] Bell and Zulueta-Fülscher, 2016, pp. 21–30.

in the combined processes of peacemaking and constitution-making "must be based on an ongoing analysis of the extent to which there is sufficient political agreement underlying each stage of the process."[115]

Bell and Zulueta-Füscher's central insight is that for societies negotiating an end to a violent conflict, both peace agreements and constitutional settlements are "part of a more complex process of achieving a political settlement," defined as "an agreed understanding of how power is to be held and exercised."[116] The broader political settlement process is often a nonlinear one, which is why the sequencing and the relationship between peace agreements and new or revised constitutions are variable. In the end, reaching a stable political settlement is what enables lasting peace. Both the peace agreement and constitutional settlement, therefore, should be seen as means rather than their own ends.

Even within each of the four pathways that lead toward a new constitutional settlement, agreements differ in their approaches to two important issues: the degree of detail on the proposed constitutional changes and whether the constitutional change follows the procedures mandated by the existing constitution. These two points of divergence can lead to substantially different constitutional processes.

How Detailed Are the Proposed Changes to the Constitution?

The agreements we reviewed can be classified in three categories, based on the level of detail that they provide about the new or revised constitution. First, a few agreements include the text of the new constitution or constitutional amendments in the agreement itself. This is uncommon, but negotiating parties have reached peace agreements and constitutional settlements at the same time in some cases. Most prominently, the full text of a new constitution for Bosnia was included as part of the Dayton Agreement.[117] Rather than present an entirely

---

[115] Bell and Zulueta-Fülscher, 2016, p. 7.

[116] Bell and Zulueta-Fülscher, 2016, pp. 16–17.

[117] Dayton Agreement, 1995, Annex 4. For caution on drawing lessons from the Bosnia model of simultaneous peacemaking and constitution-making, see Laurel E. Miller, "Designing Constitution-Making Processes: Lessons from the Past, Questions for the Future," in

new constitution, Macedonia's Ohrid Agreement included the text of several constitutional amendments that were to be "presented to the Assembly immediately" for "adoption . . . within 45 days of signature" of the agreement.[118]

Second, some agreements include ideas for a new constitutional arrangement or principles that must underpin it, but they do not specify the content or text of the constitution. Most frequently, these agreements mandate that the new constitution must contain protections of basic rights. Cambodia's Paris Agreement, for example, in a section titled "Principles for a New Constitution for Cambodia," states that

> the constitution will contain a declaration of fundamental rights, including the rights to life, personal liberty, security, freedom of movement, freedom of religion, assembly and association including political parties and trade unions, due process and equality before the law, protection from arbitrary deprivation of property or deprivation of private property without just compensation, and freedom from racial, ethnic, religious or sexual discrimination.[119]

And the Arusha Agreement for Burundi requires, among other things, "[a]doption of constitutional provisions embodying the principle of separation of powers (executive, legislative and judicial), pursuant to the provisions of Protocol II to the Agreement."[120]

Third, some agreements call for constitutional reform, and might even establish a process for the reform, but do not provide any content. The peace agreement in Tajikistan, for instance, gives the Commission on National Reconciliation the mandate to submit "to a nationwide referendum of [sic] proposals for amendments and additions to the

---

Laurel E. Miller, ed., *Framing the State in Times of Transition: Case Studies in Constitution Making*, Washington, D.C.: U.S. Institute of Peace Press, 2010, pp. 642–643.

118 Ohrid Agreement, 2001, Art. 8. The amendments are provided in Annex A of the agreement.

119 Paris Peace Agreements, 1991, Annex 5, Art. 2.

120 Burundian Arusha Accords, 2000, Protocol I, Ch. II, Art. 5, Sec. 5.

existing Constitution."[121] Nothing more is said about constitutional changes in the agreement.

Dealing with the Existing Process for Constitutional Change

In seeking constitutional reform in the aftermath of violence, peace negotiators and constitution-makers must grapple with the question of the legal basis for their actions. Under normal circumstances, constitutional changes occur under the rules set by the existing constitution. But extreme circumstances, such as severe violence or a political revolution, can render the constitution that is in place unacceptable to many or most political actors. As Brandt et al. explain, "Usually it is the institutions, the distribution of power, and the access to resources that are unacceptable, but sometimes even the existing document cannot be tolerated—perhaps because of who made it—even if the new institutions may not differ much from the old."[122] This latter situation could be the case in Afghanistan, where the Taliban consider the 2004 Constitution illegitimate. The basis for this position, at least as held by Taliban political leadership, is that the current constitution "was devised under the auspices of a 'foreign occupation' and by a state 'in the service of foreign powers' and security forces dominated by their harshest enemies."[123] Amplifying this view is the fact that the Taliban were excluded from the 2004 constitutional process. Thus, Taliban concerns might be focused less on the content of the constitution than its provenance (though their substantive views on the constitution are as yet unstated).

When the existing constitution is not acceptable, countries have come up with several methods for dealing with the prescribed procedures for changing the constitution. The first method, used in South

---

121 Government of Tajikistan and United Tajik Opposition, Protocol on the Main Functions and Powers of the Commission on National Reconciliation, Moscow, Russia, December 23, 1996a.

122 Michele Brandt et al., *Constitution-Making and Reform: Options for the Process*, Geneva, Switzerland: Interpeace, November 2011, p. 36. This section draws on the analysis in Brandt et al., 2011, Ch. 2.1, "Tasks—Starting a Process."

123 Osman and Gopal, 2016, p. 19. See also Voice of Jihad, "Transcript of Speech Delivered by Delegation of Islamic Emirate at Moscow Conference," November 9, 2018.

Africa, is to work through the processes of the existing constitution, despite its illegitimacy in the eyes of the majority. Thus, South Africa followed the procedures required by the Apartheid-era constitution to negotiate an interim constitution. The constitution-makers then followed the new rules for constitutional change established by the interim document to adopt the final constitution of 1996. The South African constitution-makers felt that following the letter of the law at each step "would give a solid legal foundation" to the final post-Apartheid constitution.[124]

The South African model is not appropriate in all cases, however. Other situations require a more dramatic break from the past. In fact, note Brandt et al., "In countries emerging from conflict, some departure from the letter of the law may be *necessary*."[125] In such cases, it is often the peace agreement itself that provides the procedures for a new constitution. The most direct method, employed in Bosnia (as mentioned earlier), is to include the new constitution in the peace agreement. In adopting a new constitution for Bosnia, the Dayton Agreement did not follow the existing procedures. Rather, Article V of the agreement states, "The Parties welcome and endorse the arrangements that have been made concerning the Constitution of Bosnia and Herzegovina, as set forth in Annex 4. The Parties shall fully respect and promote fulfillment of the commitments made therein." The constitution, as it reads in Annex 4, likewise explains its own adoption: "This Constitution shall enter into force upon signature of the General Framework Agreement [the peace agreement] as a constitutional act amending and superseding the Constitution of the Republic of Bosnia and Herzegovina."[126]

A second option is for the peace agreement to provide new procedures for constitutional change without stipulating the content of the new constitution. This was the method used in the Bonn Agreement

[124] Brandt et al., 2011, p. 51. See also p. 36.

[125] Brandt et al., 2011, p. 53. Our emphasis.

[126] Dayton Agreement, 1995, Art. V and Annex 4, Art. XII, Sec. 1.

that led to the passage of Afghanistan's current constitution.[127] Bonn set up its own extra-constitutional process for adopting a new constitution: "A Constitutional Loya Jirga shall be convened within eighteen months of the establishment of the Transitional Authority, in order to adopt a new constitution for Afghanistan."[128]

In their review of constitutional reform efforts in postconflict countries, Brandt et al. conclude that the legal framework for any changes should be thoughtfully designed so that the new document is considered valid and has legitimacy in the eyes of important stakeholders. Ultimately, however, "[o]nce a new constitution is adopted, it is unlikely that it will be attacked for lack of legal validity."[129] That radical circumstances necessitated radical change is likely to be widely acknowledged, and extra-constitutional procedures for the sake of reaching a constitutional settlement—and ultimately a political settlement—will, especially if successful, be accepted.

Monitoring and Verification

Mechanisms for the monitoring and verification of the peace agreement as a whole or for specific provisions are a way to decrease the uncertainty about whether or not the other party is actually compliant. They are a means of sharing otherwise private information and reducing the otherwise strong incentives to misrepresent that information. Political scientists Michaela Mattes and Burcu Savun label them

---

[127] Note that the Bonn Agreement also did something similar to the Dayton Agreement by establishing a new constitution in the text of the agreement itself. However, unlike the Dayton Agreement, the Bonn Agreement did not negotiate a new constitution but rather declared that the 1964 Afghan constitution, stripped of its monarchical provisions and anything else inconsistent with the agreement, would be "applicable on an interim basis until the adoption of the new Constitution" by the Constitutional Loya Jirga; Agreement on Provisional Arrangements in Afghanistan Pending the Re-Establishment of Permanent Government Institutions ("Bonn Agreement"), 2001, Art. II, Sec. 1.

[128] Bonn Agreement, 2001, Art. I, Sec. 6. For details on Afghanistan's constitutional process in 2003–2004, see J. Alexander Thier, "Big Tent, Small Tent: The Making of a Constitution in Afghanistan," in Laurel E. Miller, ed., *Framing the State in Times of Transition: Case Studies in Constitution Making*, Washington, D.C.: U.S. Institute of Peace Press, 2010.

[129] Brandt et al., 2011, p. 53.

"uncertainty-reducing provisions" and find that approximately 60 percent of agreements feature at least one.[130]

Monitoring and verification mechanisms in the agreements reviewed generally hew to one of three forms: international bodies, joint commissions with domestic parties, or joint commissions with domestic and international parties.[131] Many agreements put the responsibility for monitoring and verifying implementation entirely in the hands of an international third party, frequently the United Nations. For instance, Papua New Guinea's Lincoln Agreement calls for the United Nations Security Council to appoint "a special observer mission to monitor these arrangements."[132] And Sudan's Comprehensive Peace Agreement states, "The Parties agree to request the United Nations to constitute a lean, effective, sustainable and affordable UN Peace Support Mission to monitor and verify this Agreement and to support the implementation of the Comprehensive Peace Agreement as provided for under Chapter VI of the UN Charter."[133] In addition to the United Nations, agreements also establish third-party monitoring and verification mechanisms under the authority of multilateral bodies, such as the Organization of the Islamic Conference[134] (e.g., in the Philippines) and Organization of African Unity (e.g., in Rwanda).[135]

The most common form for monitoring and verification, however, is a joint commission with members representing all the major

---

130 Michaela Mattes and Burcu Savun, "Information, Agreement Design, and the Durability of Civil War Settlements," *American Journal of Political Science*, Vol. 54, No. 2, April 2010, p. 518.

131 Joint commissions were previously discussed in the context of foreign troop withdrawal and power-sharing in security institutions. This section covers more-general uses of the mechanism.

132 Government of Papua New Guinea and Bougainville Interim Government, Lincoln Agreement on Peace Security and Development on Bougainville, Lincoln, New Zealand, January 23, 1998, Art. 5, Sec. 5.2.

133 Comprehensive Peace Agreement (Sudan), 2005, Annexure I, Part I, Art. 15, Sec. 15.1.

134 The organization was later renamed the Organization of Islamic Cooperation.

135 Mindanao Final Agreement, 1996, Art. 12; N'sele Ceasefire Agreement, 1992, Art. III.

parties to the agreement.[136] Some joint commissions are composed entirely of domestic parties; more often, there are international members as well. An exclusively domestic joint commission was established, for example, in the Chittagong Hills Tract (Bangladesh). This "Implementation Committee" had three members, including the head of the rebel group and someone nominated by the prime minister of Bangladesh, and was given the "aim to observe the implementation process of this agreement."[137] Joint commissions that include external actors are found in a variety of agreements, such as Mozambique's Rome Accords, Angola's Lusaka Protocol, and Liberia's Accra Agreement.[138] The Accra Agreement actually created two such commissions, the Joint Verification Team and the Joint Monitoring Committee, each with representatives from the parties to the accord, ECOWAS, the United Nations, the African Union, and the International Contact Group on Liberia. Mozambique and Angola did not limit external participation to international organizations and invited individual foreign governments to join their joint commissions as well.

The role of external actors in these monitoring and verification mechanisms demonstrates that the international community can play an important role even in the absence of a peacekeeping or peace enforcement mission. Caspersen finds that international actors' involvement in postagreement implementation is more frequently "limited" than robust.[139] Only five of the 20 agreements she analyzed had armed peacekeeping missions.[140] However, even limited roles played by multilateral organizations or foreign governments, such as helping to monitor troop demobilization or verify the number and locations of weapons caches, can be beneficial for implementation. As Mattes and Savun conclude, "third parties may still play a central role in maintain-

[136] Joshi, Lee, and Mac Ginty, 2017, pp. 999–1000.

[137] People's Republic of Bangladesh and United People's Party of the Chittagong Hill Tracts, Chittagong Hill Tracts Peace Accord, Dhaka, Bangladesh, December 2, 1997, Art. A, Sec. 3.

[138] Rome Accords, 1992, Protocol I, Art. 5; Lusaka Protocol, 1994, Annex 4, Sec. 6; Accra Comprehensive Peace Agreement, 2003, Annex 1, paras. 3 and 6.

[139] Caspersen, 2017, p. 174.

[140] Caspersen, 2017, p. 42.

ing peace after civil wars even if they are unwilling or unable to act as security guarantors."[141] This finding has relevance for Afghanistan, where postagreement establishment of a robust international presence to help guarantee the peace is unlikely.

Implementation

A peace agreement, no matter how carefully negotiated, is unlikely to bring peace if its terms are not implemented. In fact, many peace processes collapse at the implementation stage as one or both parties fail to live up to their commitments. Collapse is not an unsurprising outcome for a period often marked by severe insecurity, uncertainty, mutual mistrust, and lingering disputes over core grievances; thus, overcoming these challenges requires sustained effort. Elements of the agreement itself, however, can aid in this work. "Built-in safeguards" can be included to create institutions and methods for attempting to ensure that the agreement is implemented as intended and that bumps along the road do not derail the whole process.[142] Two common safeguards in contemporary peace agreements are monitoring and verification mechanisms, discussed above, and dispute resolution mechanisms.[143] This section examines how recent agreements have established dispute resolution mechanisms as a means to increase the credibility of each party's commitments.

Disputes between the parties are practically inevitable in the post-agreement implementation phase. Thus, it is important for the agreement to establish processes and institutions for settling these problems so that they do not "disrupt the accord or even risk a resumption of fully-fledged armed conflict."[144] Such mechanisms give the parties a method for dealing with violations of the terms of the agreement, such as isolated ceasefire violations, as well as for resolving differences in interpretations of the agreement. As with monitoring and verification,

---

[141] Mattes and Savun, 2010, p. 523.

[142] Joshi, Lee, and Mac Ginty, 2017.

[143] Joshi, Lee, and Mac Ginty, 2017, also includes transitional power-sharing as a common implementation safeguard, but we discuss it separately.

[144] Joshi, Lee, and Mac Ginty, 2017, p. 999.

a frequent dispute resolution mechanism is a joint commission that brings together representatives from the government, the rebels, and, in some cases, external actors. Several agreements use the same joint commission to monitor and verify implementation and to resolve disputes between the parties. For example, the Implementation Monitoring Committee established by the Arusha Accords for Burundi was mandated to

> (a) Follow up, monitor, supervise, coordinate and ensure the effective implementation of all the provisions of the Agreement;
>
> b) Ensure that the implementation timetable is respected;
>
> (c) Ensure the accurate interpretation of the Agreement;
>
> (d) Reconcile points of view;
>
> (e) Arbitrate and rule on any dispute that may arise among the signatories.[145]

Likewise, Mozambique's Supervisory and Monitoring Commission was a joint body with representatives of the government, rebels, United Nations, Organization of African Unity, and "countries to be agreed upon by the Parties" that was tasked to "guarantee the implementation of the provisions" as well as "assume responsibility for the authentic interpretation of the agreements" and "settle any disputes that may arise between the Parties."[146]

Other agreements created independent dispute resolution mechanisms. The 2002 agreement between Indonesia and the Free Aceh Movement established a Joint Council, composed of "the most senior representatives" of the government and the Free Aceh Movement,

[145] Burundian Arusha Accords, 2000, Protocol V, Art. 3, Sec. 1. Protocol V, Art. 3, Sec. 2.a of the agreement provides the required membership for the committee: "Two representatives of the Parties; One representative of the Government; Six Burundians designated for their moral integrity; [and] Representatives of: The United Nations; The Organization of African Unity; [and] The regional Peace Initiative on Burundi."

[146] Rome Accords, 1992, Protocol V, Art. I, Secs. 2 and 5.

whose "function . . . will be to resolve all issues or disputes arising out of the implementation of this Agreement."[147] In addition to joint commissions, other dispute resolution mechanisms include a "Council of Elders and Religious Leaders" created to settle "conflicting differences of interpretation" of the Lomé Agreement in Sierra Leone; a "constitutional council" established in Lebanon's Taif Accords "to interpret the constitution, to observe the constitutionality of the laws, and to settle disputes and contests emanating from presidential and parliamentary elections"; and the Bougainville Agreement's provision that the governments of Papua New Guinea and Bougainville "will try to resolve disputes by consultation, or, where required, through mediation or arbitration. . . . [And if that fails,] then it may be taken to court."[148]

Transitional Justice

At the end of any conflict, competing impulses are evident: the desire to move on and the desire for justice. This could be true in Afghanistan, where the numbers of perpetrators and victims of violence are great. In recent history, Afghan peacemaking attempts have not emphasized transitional justice. The 1993 Islamabad Accord featured the "immediate and unconditional release" of prisoners, the 2016 agreement with Gulbuddin Hekmatyar "guarantee[d] judicial immunity [to] the leader and members of Hizb-e Islami" and "committed to the release of [their] prisoners and detainees," and Afghan President Ashraf Ghani's February 28, 2018, offer of peace to the Taliban proposed a prisoner release as well as other concessions that amount to a de facto amnesty.[149] Thus, this section examines amnesty and prisoner release in peace

---

[147] Government of the Republic of Indonesia and the Free Aceh Movement, Cessation of Hostilities Framework Agreement, December 9, 2002, Art. 8.

[148] Lomé Peace Agreement, 1999, Art. VIII; Taif Accords, 1989, Art. III, Sec. B, para. 2; Government of Papua New Guinea and Bougainville Interim Provincial Government, Bougainville Peace Agreement, Arawa, Bougainville, Papua New Guinea, August 30, 2001, Art. B, Sec. 11, paras. 265–266.

[149] Islamabad Accord, 1993, Art. 5; Government of the Islamic Republic of Afghanistan and Hizb-e Islami of Afghanistan, Agreement, Kabul, Afghanistan, September 22, 2016, Art. 11; Government of the Islamic Republic of Afghanistan, "Offering Peace: Framing the Kabul Conference of February 28, 2018," February 28, 2018, p. 3. Afghanistan also enacted a law

agreements, which scholars find tend to appear together (often with combatant reintegration as well) in post–Cold War settlements, rather than tribunals, truth commissions, or other such instruments.[150]

Amnesty

Amnesties are widely condemned by the human rights community but repeatedly feature in peace agreements.[151] This is because the perpetrators of abuses are unlikely to come to the negotiating table or commit to peaceful politics if they believe they will be prosecuted for their past actions. Providing important players with immunity from retribution, however unpalatable, is seen as "an indispensable tool in reaching peace settlements when perpetrators remain strong."[152]

This reasoning is often explicitly stated in the agreement itself. By providing a justification for amnesty clauses—something typically not done for other clauses in the agreements reviewed—the drafters are implicitly acknowledging that it is a controversial decision that many will oppose. As a result, agreements frequently state that amnesty is being granted in order "to consolidate the peace and promote the cause of national reconciliation," "to reduce tensions and divisions that could continue to flow from the conflict," "to advance such reconciliation and reconstruction," or "to promote forgiveness and national reconciliation and to restore social cohesion and solidarity."[153]

---

in 2008 providing a general amnesty for the period preceding the post-2001 Interim Administration (National Reconciliation, General Amnesty, and National Stability Law, Official Gazette, 13 Qaus 1387, Serial No. 965.)

[150] Leslie Vinjamuri and Aaron P. Boesenecker, *Accountability and Peace Agreements: Mapping Trends from 1980 to 2006*, Geneva, Switzerland: Centre for Humanitarian Dialogue, September 2007, pp. 21–23.

[151] In agreements ending both civil and interstate wars signed between 1980 and 2006, amnesties were the most common justice mechanism, featuring in 30 of 77 agreements; Vinjamuri and Boesenecker, 2007, p. 16.

[152] Jack Snyder and Leslie Vinjamuri, "Trials and Errors: Principle and Pragmatism in Strategies of International Justice," *International Security*, Vol. 28, No. 3, Winter 2003/2004, p. 39.

[153] Abidjan Accords, 1996, Art. 14; Lomé Peace Agreement, 1999, Art. IX; Bougainville Peace Agreement, 2001, Art. F, Sec. 3(a), para. 340(c); Interim Constitution (South Africa), 1994, "National Unity and Reconciliation"; Republic of Côte d'Ivoire and Forces Nou-

The primary distinction among amnesties is their scope—that is, whether they grant general amnesty or limit the amnesty based on the severity of the crime.[154] Universal amnesties were granted to combatants in several of the peace agreements reviewed. The Abidjan Agreement, for example, states, "the Government of Sierra Leone shall ensure that no official or judicial action is taken against any member of the RUF/SL [Revolutionary United Front/Sierra Leone] in respect of anything done by them in pursuit of their objectives as members of that organization up to the time of the signing of this Agreement."[155] In the Lomé Agreement, signed three years later, Sierra Leone's government again guaranteed amnesties: "absolute and free pardon and reprieve to all combatants and collaborators." This agreement also specified "absolute and free pardon" for the leader of the RUF as well as "immunity to former combatants, exiles and other persons, currently outside the country for reasons related to the armed conflict."[156]

Other agreements exclude perpetrators of extreme crimes from their amnesties. For example, the Dayton Agreement prohibits amnesty for "a serious violation of international humanitarian law as defined in the Statute of the International [Criminal] Tribunal for the Former Yugoslavia since January 1, 1991," and the Arusha Agreement in Burundi excludes "acts of genocide, crimes against humanity or war crimes."[157] Because of the establishment of the International Criminal Court in 2002, peace negotiators are now less likely than in the past to provide amnesty for the most serious war crimes. As transitional justice expert Leslie Vinjamuri concludes, "Formal amnesties that explicitly refer to international crimes are now widely acknowledged to be off

---

velles de Côte d'Ivoire, Ouagadougou Political Agreement, Ouagadougou, Burkina Faso, March 4, 2007, Art. VI, Sec. 6.3.

[154] From 1980 to 2006, general amnesties were more common than limited amnesties (present in 22 agreements versus eight); Vinjamuri and Boesenecker, 2007, p. 16.

[155] Abidjan Accords, 1996, Art. 14.

[156] Lomé Peace Agreement, 1999, Art. IX.

[157] Dayton Agreement, 1995, Annex 7, Art. VI; Burundian Arusha Accords, 2000, Protocol V, Art. 26, Sec. 1 (l).

the table."[158] Both the Bosnia and Burundi agreements also illustrate how some other types of crimes can be exempted from immunity: The Dayton Agreement excludes "common crime[s] unrelated to the conflict" and Burundi excludes "participation in coups d'etat" from the declared amnesty.[159]

Prisoner Release

Provisions for the release of conflict-related prisoners are generally quite similar to one another and were common in the agreements reviewed.[160] First, there is wide agreement over who is to be released: prisoners of war and/or political prisoners. In all of the agreements that include prisoner release, except for in Northern Ireland and Bosnia, the release is unconditionally applied to "all political prisoners and prisoners of war," as Sierra Leone's Abidjan Agreement puts it.[161] Both the Good Friday Agreement and Dayton Agreement place conditions on their prisoner releases, but their logic for the restrictions are very different. In Northern Ireland, "Prisoners affiliated to organisations which have not established or are not maintaining a complete and unequivocal ceasefire will not benefit from the arrangements."[162] In Bosnia, prisoners who had been "reasonably suspected" of international crimes by the International Criminal Tribunal for the Former Yugoslavia were not to be released.[163]

There is also general consensus among the agreements that the time frame for release is quick and that there should be international verification. Many peace agreements guarantee "immediate" release, and nearly all of them commit to releasing prisoners in one month or

[158] Leslie Vinjamuri, "The Distant Promise of a Negotiated Justice," *Daedalus*, Vol. 146, No. 1, Winter 2017, p. 101.

[159] Dayton Agreement, 1995, Annex 7, Art. VI; Burundian Arusha Accords, 2000, Protocol V, Art. 26, Sec. 1 (l).

[160] Vinjamuri and Boesenecker, 2007, p. 19, finds that prisoner releases are the second most common justice mechanism (26 of 77 agreements have them).

[161] Abidjan Accords, 1996, Art. 19.

[162] Good Friday Agreement, 1998, "Prisoners," para. 2.

[163] Dayton Agreement, 1995, Annex 1-A, Art. IX, Sec. 1 (g).

less. Not all of the agreements with prisoner release include a verification mechanism, but of those that do, all but one request the International Committee of the Red Cross to verify and/or assist with the release of prisoners. The exception is the agreement in Tajikistan, which arranges for domestic monitoring, to be conducted by the President and Commission on National Reconciliation.[164]

Property and Land Conflicts

Land and property disputes are an important driver of conflict in Afghanistan and are likely to be exacerbated in the aftermath of an agreement as refugees and displaced people return home and as power relationships in some areas of the country realign. The land problem in Afghanistan is multidimensional, and any agreement might need to deal with several different sources of conflict, including population growth, forced migration, urbanization, the rising value of land, lack of documentation, and corruption. The Afghanistan Research and Evaluation Unit (AREU) distinguishes five types of land conflicts:

1. Conflicts involving the illegal occupation of land by powerful people;
2. Conflicts involving inheritance rights to private property;
3. Conflicts involving the return of people to land they previously owned;
4. Conflicts over private property between established villagers (not returnees, refugees or internally displaced people);
5. Conflicts involving common property resources managed through common property regimes, for instance certain pastures, forests and water for irrigation.[165]

These different types of disputes call for different solutions. But any solution to land conflicts must also account for two features of con-

---

164 Government of Tajikistan and United Tajik Opposition, Statute of the Commission on National Reconciliation, Moscow, Russia, December 23, 1996b, Art. III, Sec. 7.

165 Colin Deschamps and Alan Roe, *Land Conflict in Afghanistan: Building Capacity to Address Vulnerability*, Kabul, Afghanistan: Afghanistan Research and Evaluation Unit, April 2009, p. xii.

temporary Afghanistan. First is the limited ability of the central state to address the problems "given [its] limited presence, poor enforcement capability, bad reputation (due to corruption and land grabbing), and the widespread lack of authentic title deeds."[166] Second is the prevalence of communally held land. This type of land cannot simply be titled to an individual, and thus many potential solutions rooted in the protection of private property rights cannot be neatly applied. The AREU suggests instead that a solution should "recognize shared 'rights of use' rather than 'ownership' of common property."[167]

A Right to Property

A common approach to issues related to land and property in peace agreements is to ground them in the language of rights, specifically the right to property. Several agreements place "the right to property" in their enumerations of the "human rights and fundamental freedoms" guaranteed to people in the postconflict society.[168] Others place the right to property in their provisions on land and property (e.g., Colombia).[169] In addition to the basic right to property, several other property-related rights are provided by agreements. For instance, the Dayton Agreement guarantees "the right to liberty of movement and residence"; the parties to an agreement in Myanmar agreed to "avoid forcibly taking . . . property . . . from civilians" and "avoid the destruction of public property, looting, theft, or the taking of property without permission"; and an agreement in Nepal established the right to

---

[166] Erica Gaston and Lilian Dang, "Addressing Land Conflict in Afghanistan," Washington, D.C.: U.S. Institute of Peace, June 2015, p. 1.

[167] Deschamps and Roe, 2009, p. xiv.

[168] Both quotations appear verbatim in Dayton Agreement, 1995, Annex 4, Art. II, Sec. 12 (k); and Government of Sudan, South Sudan United Democratic Salvation Front, et al., The Sudan Peace Agreement ("Khartoum Peace Agreement"), Khartoum, Sudan, April 21, 1997, Ch. 3, "Fundamental Rights and Freedoms," Sec. 5.

[169] Government of Colombia and Revolutionary Armed Forces of Colombia, Final Agreement to End the Armed Conflict and Build a Stable and Lasting Peace, Bogota, Colombia, November 24, 2016, Ch. 1, "Principles."

housing and "the freedom to choose within legal norms the location of one's residence."[170]

The Return of Displaced Persons

The property problem most often addressed in the reviewed peace agreements is displaced persons returning to their former homes to find that they have been occupied by someone else. In this situation, most agreements give the right to the property to the original owner or occupant. The draft Rambouillet Agreement, for instance, "recognize[s] that all persons have the right to return to their homes . . . [and] the right to reoccupy their real property, assert their occupancy rights in state-owned property, and recover their other property and personal possessions."[171] The Dayton Agreement states, "All refugees and displaced persons have the right freely to return to their homes of origin. They have the right . . . to have restored to them property of which they were deprived in the course of hostilities since 1991."[172] Similar guarantees were made to returning displaced persons in Eastern Slavonia ("the right to have restored to them any property that was taken from them by unlawful acts or that they were forced to abandon"), Nepal ("the right of the people displaced by the conflict and their families to return back to their homes or to settle in any other location of their choice"), Liberia ("Refugees or internally displaced persons, desirous of returning to their original Counties or permanent residences, shall be assisted to do so"), and Mozambique ("Mozambican refugees and displaced persons shall be guaranteed restitution of property owned by them which is still in existence and the right to take

[170] Dayton Agreement, 1995, Annex 4, Art. II, Sec. 12 (m); Government of the Republic of the Union of Myanmar and the Ethnic Armed Organizations, The Nationwide Ceasefire Agreement, Naypyidaw, Myanmar, October 15, 2015, Ch. 3, Arts. 9 (d) and (g); Government of Nepal and Communist Party of Nepal (Maoist), Comprehensive Peace Accord, Kathmandu, Nepal, November 21, 2006, Ch. 7, Art. 3, Sec. 3.

[171] Rambouillet Agreement, 1999, Art. II, Sec. 3.

[172] Dayton Agreement, 1995, Annex 4, Art. II, Sec. 14.

legal action to secure the return of such property from individuals in possession of it").[173]

The right to restitution, however, is not universally guaranteed. The Rwandan Arusha Accords in fact explicitly denies the right in many cases. It begins by stating, "Each person who returns shall be free to settle down in any place of their choice inside the country, so long as they do not encroach upon the rights of other people." But then the agreement restricts the application of this provision only to displaced persons from the previous ten years. As the agreement puts it, "in order to promote social harmony and national reconciliation, refugees who left the country more than 10 years ago should not reclaim their properties, which might have been occupied by other people." Instead, the government is to "compensate them by putting land at their disposal and shall help them to resettle."[174]

Croatia also abridged the right to return home. As a 2018 report by Displacement Solutions and the Norwegian Refugee Council explains, Croatia's Programme of Return and Accommodation of Expellees, Displaced Persons and Refugees contained two provisions that prevented many people from returning. First, "the return of property was [in practice] predicated on the availability and acceptability of alternative accommodation for the current secondary occupant, thus leaving former holders of occupancy rights in many instances, without a restitution remedy." And second, "Only owners of private property were entitled to benefit from the restitution procedure, despite the fact that many seeking restitution were classified as 'social occupants' holding social occupancy rights, a status somewhere between outright owner-

[173] Government of Croatia and Serb Negotiating Delegation, Basic Agreement on the Region of Eastern Slavonia, Baranja and Western Sirmium ("Erdut Agreement"), Erdut, Croatia, and Zagreb, Croatia, November 12, 1995, Art. 8; Comprehensive Peace Accord (Nepal), 2006, Ch. 7, Art. 3, Sec. 3; Accra Comprehensive Peace Agreement, 2003, Art. XXX, Sec. 1 (b); Rome Accords, 1992, Protocol III, Art. IV (e).

[174] Government of the Republic of Rwanda and the Rwandese Patriotic Front, Protocol of Agreement on the Repatriation of Rwandese Refugees and the Resettlement of Displaced Persons, Arusha, Tanzania, June 9, 1993a, Art. 4. Many Rwandan refugees who returned in the 1990s had fled as early as 1959, well over ten years prior to the signing of the agreement.

ship and tenancy."[175] As a result, many Croatians were denied the ability to return to their prewar homes.

Yet even the agreements that protect the right of displaced persons to return home and have their property restored acknowledge that it is not always possible to do so. Over the course of a conflict, some homes will be destroyed, requisitioned by the government, or subject to some other circumstance that prevents return by the prewar occupant or owner. In most cases, the agreement arranges for compensation to the victim. For instance, the Dayton Agreement gives "all refugees and displaced persons . . . the right . . . to be compensated for any such property that cannot be restored to them."[176] And the agreement in Eastern Slavonia specifies that there should be "just compensation" and states that "the right to . . . receive compensation for property that cannot be returned and to receive assistance in reconstruction of damaged property shall be equally available to all persons without regard to ethnicity."[177]

Lack of Documentation

Another land issue dealt with by several peace agreements is the lack of documentation for land ownership. In Afghanistan, "no more than 20 percent of the land . . . is accurately titled," which makes documentation a key problem in land disputes.[178] Our review of the agreements suggests three general approaches to addressing the issue: case-by-case methods, land surveys, and legislative solutions.

The first approach is to establish mechanisms to ease the resolution of disputes on a case-by-case basis. In Kosovo, this meant "issuing necessary documents" to facilitate the return of refugees.[179] Mozambique passed a law (separate from the peace agreement) that required

[175] Displacement Solutions and Norwegian Refugee Council, *Housing, Land and Property Rights and Peace Agreements: Guidance for the Myanmar Peace Process*, February 2018, p. 20.

[176] Dayton Agreement, 1995, Annex 4, Art. II, Sec. 14.

[177] Erdut Agreement, 1995, Arts. 8 and 9.

[178] Gaston and Dang, 2015, p. 1.

[179] Rambouillet Agreement, 1999, Art. II, Sec. 3.

courts to accept oral testimony in place of documentary evidence of land ownership.[180]

The second approach, adopted in El Salvador, Guatemala, Bangladesh, and Colombia, is to undertake a national approach to land documentation, either by conducting a general land survey or through the blanket legalization of irregular land claims. In the Colombia Agreement, the government committed to launching a "comprehensive and multi-purpose General Cadastral Information System, which . . . leads to the creation and updating of the rural cadaster." Colombia also emphasized the legal titling of untitled land "with a view to legalising and protecting rights pertaining to small and medium-sized rural properties, in other words, guaranteeing the rights of people who are the legitimate owners and holders of the land." The plan is for the government to "progressively title, subject to constitutional and legal provisions, all properties occupied or held by the rural population in Colombia."[181]

The third approach is to overhaul national laws dealing with land ownership. This model was most clearly used by El Salvador, which, because of the recognition that "the current agrarian legislation is haphazard, contradictory and incomplete," agreed to "submit the relevant draft legislation to the Legislative Assembly" so that the laws could be "harmonized and unified into an agrarian code."[182]

Independent Commissions

Establishing an independent commission to adjudicate land or property disputes is a common mechanism established in agreements. The Chittagong Hill Tracts Peace Accord, for example, provides that "A commission (land commission) headed by a retired justice shall be formed for settling land disputes."[183] In El Salvador, "a special com-

---

[180] Displacement Solutions and Norwegian Refugee Council, 2018, p. 21. This law, the Land Law of 1997, was passed after the agreement was signed.

[181] Final Agreement to End the Armed Conflict and Build a Stable and Lasting Peace (Colombia), 2016, Ch. 1, Art. 1, Secs. 9 and 5.

[182] Chapultepec Peace Agreement, 1992, Ch. V, Art. 2 (F).

[183] Chittagong Hill Tracts Peace Accord, 1997, Art. D, Sec. 4.

mission whose members shall be of recognized integrity and ability . . . [was] to facilitate the settlement of disputes between current holders and rightful owners."[184] In Bosnia, a "Commission shall receive and decide any claims for real property . . . , where the property has not voluntarily been sold or otherwise transferred since April 1, 1992, and where the claimant does not now enjoy possession of that property."[185] There were two commissions established in Kosovo, one for residential property and a second for commercial property. The residential commission, the Housing and Property Directorate, was also established to "co-ordinate housing law and policy."[186]

Land Reform

Land reform is an important issue in several agreements, particularly when the conflict was fueled by peasant mobilization, such as in Colombia, El Salvador, Guatemala, and Nepal. However, it does not appear to be a key demand of the Afghan parties, and so we only mention it in passing. In the Colombia agreement, the most recent major peace agreement reached in the world as of this writing, land reform is a central feature. The parties agreed to the creation of a Land Fund that would give free land to "small-scale farmer communities and especially rural women without land or with insufficient land and the rural communities most affected by poverty, neglect and the conflict."[187] Much of the long text of the agreement is dedicated to explaining the details of this plan.

Conclusion

To inform the drafting of a potential peace agreement for Afghanistan, we looked outward in this chapter to agreements ending conflicts in other countries around the world. We examined how these agreements devised solutions to eight key and/or controversial issues in the Afghan

---

[184] Chapultepec Peace Agreement, 1992, Ch. V, Arts. 3 (D) and 3 (D) (b).

[185] Dayton Agreement, 1995, Annex 7, Art. XI.

[186] Displacement Solutions and Norwegian Refugee Council, 2018, p. 18.

[187] Final Agreement to End the Armed Conflict and Build a Stable and Lasting Peace (Colombia), 2016, Ch. 1, Art. 1, Sec. 1.

context: political power-sharing, withdrawal of foreign troops, military power-sharing, ceasefire, constitutional reform, implementation and enforcement, transitional justice, and property and land disputes. We examined the elements of the negotiated settlements to these issues, seeking commonalities and differences among the agreements to identify options for Afghanistan.

The broad search for ideas we conducted proved valuable for our purposes. Some of the ideas might work in Afghanistan and were included in our agreement or noted as possible alternatives to our recommended solutions. Others, for any number of reasons, are not relevant, appropriate, or plausible for Afghanistan, but understanding how actors in multiple conflicts settled these crucial issues was informative nonetheless.

CHAPTER FIVE

Conclusion and Recommendations

In this chapter, we highlight important ways in which the suggested substance of our agreement in Chapter Three might satisfy some of the parties' goals, while acknowledging how some of the text in our agreement comes close to the parties' redlines. We also identify some key vulnerabilities of any agreement, no matter how closely it resembles the text we present. Finally, we offer several broad policy recommendations.

Does the Agreement Text Satisfy the Parties' Goals and Avoid Their Redlines?

As noted in Chapter Two, the conflict parties have, as of the time we prepared this report, only to a limited extent developed policies on their specific negotiating aims, positions, and acceptable fall-back options. Consequently, it is difficult to assess with certainty how well the text in our proposed agreement meets their goals and avoids crossing their redlines, particularly because both can be expected to evolve during the course of negotiations. Moreover, the text in its entirety is not likely to meet with the ready approval of any party because—as a real peace agreement will need to be—it is a compromise document, both in terms of specific provisions and of balancing between different provisions.

Nevertheless, several elements of the text would likely appeal to the parties in important respects, including the following:

- For the pro-government side, the main contours of the post-2001 democratic political system are left intact, the existing constitution is maintained as the starting point for any revisions and stays in effect until a new document is put in place, and continued support from the United States and other donors is anticipated.
- For the Taliban, the presence of U.S. and NATO forces is brought to an end; an opportunity is created for adopting a fresh constitution; a High Council of Islamic Scholars, which could be a vehicle for realizing aspects of Islamic governance, is introduced into the system of government; and sanctions removal is provided, thus signifying the political legitimization of the Taliban.
- For the United States, there are counterterrorism assurances, and there is a pathway toward ending its military involvement in Afghanistan in a manner that has some prospect of leaving stability in its wake.

In some respects, endeavoring to craft compromises required skating close to potential redlines; whether some of the proposals cross such lines depends on how the parties' positions might evolve. Elements of particular note in this regard include the following:

- The concept of an Afghanistan Support Team that enables foreign security cooperation and assistance focused on counterterrorism might not be acceptable to the Taliban because it would authorize the continued presence of some foreign forces. (The name "Afghanistan Support Team," the description of its mission and limitations, and its discontinuity with the current U.S./NATO mission were all written in a manner to underscore Afghan sovereignty and enhance the prospects of acceptability to the Taliban.) At the time that research for this report began, the United States seemed likely to try to negotiate authority for maintaining a continued counterterrorism operations capability in Afghanistan; this concept was intended to at least partially satisfy that interest. By the time this report was in the final stages, U.S. interest in maintaining such a capability was more uncertain.

- The modest degree of devolution of authority from the central to provincial level proposed in the text would not be the first choice of the Taliban or some of the factions on the pro-government side but might be a satisfactory second choice, if they see during negotiations that there are not enough assured shares of power to spread around otherwise. For Afghanistan's minority ethnic groups, at least moderate decentralization could be attractive, and for a political settlement to endure, it will be important to satisfy a broad range of interests. We cannot be sure, however, that even our quite limited proposal would not be rejected out of hand by ethnic Pashtuns in particular, for whom any suggestion of decentralization has been controversial until now.
- Similarly, the proposal to somewhat reduce the current system's extraordinary scope of presidential power might not be attractive to either the government or the Taliban (assuming the Taliban are prepared to entertain the idea of an elected president), given the insistence of both on a highly centralized system. However, it is difficult to see how to resolve opposing interests in gaining hold of maximal power without lessening the winner-take-all nature of the existing presidential system.
- The text identifies the government of the Islamic Republic of Afghanistan and the Islamic Movement of the Afghan Taliban as parties and signatories. As of this writing, the Taliban had not agreed to negotiate with the government as such (as opposed to with "other Afghans" in their supposed individual capacities as influential figures) and had not agreed to give up use of the name "Islamic Emirate of Afghanistan." Reference to the "Emirate" (the name of the former Taliban regime) is a probable redline for the pro-government side. Inability to resolve this issue along the lines suggested would be a reason to worry about the genuineness of commitment to compromise and would be difficult to square with an overall approach that maintains many of the post 2001 government institutions, laws, and system features. Alternatives such as signature by the negotiators individually or no signatures at all might be feasible but would be more appropriate for a peace agreement in a situation of complete rupture from the preceding

regime (such as the context for the 2001 Bonn Agreement, which was signed by "the participants in the UN Talks on Afghanistan").

- The agreement includes limited references to human rights and only relatively oblique references to gender (such as a provision for "equal access to education, employment, and health care"). Our expectation was that a more elaborate enumeration of rights and liberties would be better suited to the constitution than to a peace agreement. Furthermore, we judged that an ambitious approach to including rights provisions in the agreement could bog down negotiations given likely Taliban (and perhaps other) resistance. Nevertheless, our approach could be controversial.

Key Risks of Implementation Failure

The history of attempted peacemaking in Afghanistan over the last four decades is not a happy one. There are many ways in which another attempt could fail, even if negotiations result in a written agreement. Peace implementation processes following intense and protracted conflict understandably tend to be fraught in general; the research and analysis undertaken for this report illuminated several specific high-probability risks for implementation of a peace agreement in Afghanistan in particular.

Power-Sharing Could Exacerbate Afghanistan's Political Fragility

Over the past two decades, Afghan politics even without involvement of the Taliban have been fractious, political stability has been fragile, and competition for resources (in a patronage-based system) has been intense. Institutions are still weak and therefore provide little ballast for the ship of state. Introducing the Taliban into this picture in any sort of power-sharing arrangement is not likely to quickly bring greater stability. Indeed, drawing the Taliban into the political mainstream could introduce another political fault line, among Pashtuns. Afghanistan over the past two decades has already achieved a form of power-sharing in that all the major ethnic groups—Pashtun, Tajik, Uzbek, and Hazara—have been represented in elected and appointed government positions throughout that period. The Pashtun component of existing de facto power-sharing arrangements has not, of course, included the largely Pashtun Taliban. Intra-Pashtun contestation can therefore be expected to be a problematic factor in peace negotiations and especially in implementation if this contest is not resolved in an agreement. Forceful Afghan leadership and strong external support will be needed to overcome the naturally dim prospects of reaching a political settlement that is so clear and uncontested in its terms that its implementation is not threatened by chronic political instability and power struggles.

Clear Enough Transitional Security Arrangements Will Be Tough to Achieve

One of the most difficult elements to negotiate and perhaps the area of greatest implementation vulnerability will be security arrangements for the immediate aftermath of a peace agreement—regardless of whether the parties adopt a comprehensive or phased approach to concluding an agreement. If the negotiating parties and their soldiers and fighters do not have a clear understanding of who is authorized to bear arms and use force during the implementation period, any agreement could quickly unravel as a result of escalation of local disputes, purposeful spoiling, or other reasons for outbreaks of violence.

The transitional security arrangements proposed in Article II.5 of the agreement text are far from ideal. They are premised on the idea that Afghan government security institutions will need to be reconfigured in a way that brings together the existing state forces and the Taliban and that achieving that result will take some time, during which it will need to be clear what entities are responsible for security throughout the country. The proposal is further premised on the assumption that neither the Taliban nor the government forces will agree to be absorbed into the other from the moment of concluding an agreement. Therefore, we propose negotiation of a map of areas of responsibility, though we also propose several alternative options. For any of these options, negotiation will be difficult and implementation tenuous; however, we were unable to identify, and no one whom we consulted suggested, any superior ideas for how to solve this difficult problem. Indeed, no one we consulted appeared to have yet thought much about this issue at all as of the time of those discussions.

Implementation Probably Will Not Be Guaranteed by a Peacekeeping or Peace Enforcement Mission

Another significant vulnerability is likely to be the lack of a peacekeeping or peace enforcement mission to guarantee implementation of an agreement. There is as yet no evidence of international appetite for such a mission, regardless of Afghan preferences one way or another. In the absence of such a mission, the main external mechanism for enforcement would be threat of reintervention, but after nearly 20 years of foreign military intervention in Afghanistan, the political bar for reinserting forces, at least on the part of the United States and NATO, will likely be quite high. Political support for an agreement (as distinct from enforcement) on the part of regional powers and in financial terms by international donors could somewhat mitigate the lack of a hard-power guarantee of implementation. However, sustaining a coalition of support and keeping attention focused to a degree that would have a strong probability of mitigating conflict recurrence will be a considerable diplomatic challenge. Moreover, robust cooperation among the regional powers in common support for Afghanistan's stability—although not impossible—would be historically anomalous. Ultimately, the lack of external guarantors would mean that implementation will rely entirely on internal Afghan commitment to making the agreement work and the regional powers' willingness to at least avoid destructive interference.

Spoilers on All Sides Will Need to Be Contained

Related to the preceding point, means will be needed for containing spoilers internal to Afghanistan—those individuals or groups on any side of the conflict that oppose the terms and wish to see the settlement fail. There is little that any written agreement can do to address this issue directly. The main way to mitigate the risk in the negotiation phase will be to achieve the greatest extent of consensus on and genuine commitment to the settlement as possible. In the implementation phase, particularly in the absence of external involvement in ensuring implementation, each side will need to take responsibility for managing the potential spoilers within its own ranks because it will have the greatest capacity to do so. Similarly, each side will need to police those among its ranks who might attempt reprisals against their former foes.

Transitional Government and Security Arrangements Could Become Stuck

The shift from transitional to permanent government and security arrangements could stall. If, for instance, the constitutional reform process becomes deadlocked, or if controversial aspects of the political settlement are left ambiguous and resolution is deferred to the implementation phase, then the transitional governance arrangements could become stuck in place, leaving Afghanistan in a politically and institutionally weakened condition. Furthermore, because of the difficulty of reconstituting the security forces, the transitional security arrangements could remain in effect for a protracted period of time, which could harden the temporary territorial division of areas of security responsibility.

Afghanistan Will Remain Vulnerable to the Effects of Contestation Between External Actors

Building durable peace in Afghanistan will require support from—or at least noninterference on the part of—a group of countries that are not naturally close collaborators and are, in some cases, outright competitors. Aside from the United States, which will need to lead western support for implementation of a settlement, this group includes Pakistan, Iran, China, Russia, and India. Each of these countries has long had one or more favored clients within Afghanistan. When the terms of any settlement begin to emerge, these states will likely evaluate those terms relative to their own interests in advancing the positions of their Afghan clients. In addition, it is unlikely that any settlement could enjoy the wholehearted support of both Pakistan and India, which have treated Afghanistan as a theater for competition. Growing tensions between the United States and Iran could affect Iran's willingness to support a negotiated outcome influenced greatly by the United

States. But Iran will need to weigh its disinterest in falling in step with U.S. policy in Afghanistan against its interest in the stability of its neighbor.

Policy Recommendations

Beyond the specific recommendations infused in our peace agreement in Chapter Three, including its alternative options, we end with several broader policy recommendations for the internal and external negotiating parties.

Aim for a Substantive Peace Agreement, Not a Process Roadmap

As of late 2019, it was uncertain whether negotiators would aim—if peace talks among Afghans commence—to conclude a comprehensive settlement that solves the problem of power-sharing in political and security domains or aim for a more minimalist, process-oriented agreement, like the 2001 Bonn Agreement, that lays out a roadmap for eventually solving that problem. Although negotiating a substantive settlement would obviously be more difficult and time-consuming than negotiating a process roadmap, it is, in the end, the lower-risk approach. Filling in the more difficult details down the road will be harder, not easier, once international attention turns away as a result of an agreement being reached and once the United States' hard leverage associated with its military presence dissipates. Our recommendation, therefore, is to avoid being under-ambitious. Even with the level of detail suggested in our agreement text (which, in comparative terms, is far from the most complex or exhaustive), there will be many elements to flesh out during implementation—including, most significantly, the precise terms of a new or revised constitution. But the more partial an agreement is, the more fragile it is likely to be.

Link the Internal and External Aspects of a Settlement

The less intertwined the external and internal elements of an agreement are, the more fragile it is likely to be. External leverage—specifically, U.S. backing for the Afghan security forces and government and U.S.

capability to satisfy, or not, the Taliban demand for foreign military withdrawal—is a powerful variable in determining whether a political settlement can be reached and implemented. Concluding a separate peace between the United States and the Taliban, one whose terms are largely disassociated from achievement of an Afghan political settlement, would pose the risk of that bilateral accord being carried out regardless of the status of an Afghan peace process. If the expenditure of external leverage (already a wasting asset in recent years) is not tied to implementation of commitments among Afghans but instead is exhausted early on, then implementation will be less certain. As the work presented in this report proceeded, U.S. policy shifted toward accepting the Taliban's preferred bifurcation of negotiations into a U.S.-Taliban track focused on the issue of foreign troop withdrawal and a possible subsequent intra-Afghan track. Thus, the likelihood of separate agreements has increased. We have not, however, modified our recommendation that the external and internal elements should be tied together, which is reflected in the structure of our agreement text.

Draft Preferred Outcomes Early in the Negotiating Process

Each negotiating party should develop its preferred version of an agreement text early in the peace process. The results of such an exercise can provide each party with directional guidance as it negotiates toward its goals. The process of developing a preferred text can enable a party to develop internal consensus, work out the details of negotiating positions and offers, and imagine compromises. A useful approach could be to begin with identifying clear goals and guiding principles and build from there.

Provide Expert Assistance for Shaping Negotiating Positions and Compromises

The Afghan parties are currently only at the starting gates of substantive preparation for any talks that might commence. The international sponsors and supporters of a peace process who have a stake in the outcome should ensure that any help the parties might accept in transforming their goals into practical proposals and in designing compromises will be forthcoming. If and when talks among Afghan parties are set, the organizers will need to ensure that a neutral process manager prepares draft agreement text based on the parties' proposals and perhaps also on the manager's own suggested compromises.

Anticipate the Need for Donors to Help Fund Implementation

For foreign donors to Afghanistan, it will be important not to be penny-wise and pound-foolish. Growing donor fatigue with Afghanistan after two decades of extraordinary expenditures is not likely to reverse in the aftermath of a peace agreement. However, even though foreign financial support for a postagreement Afghanistan cannot guarantee successful implementation, *not* providing support adequate to help enable a new government structure to function and the reconfiguration of security forces to be effectuated would virtually guarantee implementation failure. Afghanistan remains one of the world's most impoverished countries[1] and will be hard-pressed to bankroll implementation on its own.

Moreover, Afghanistan's political landscape consists of competing patronage networks, all of which are dependent on either foreign assistance or criminal activity. Such dependence is not a new phenomenon, and history suggests that the withdrawal of foreign aid would exacerbate the competition for resources. This competition would pose one of the greatest risks of return to violent conflict.

---

1 International Monetary Fund data place Afghanistan tenth from the bottom of all countries in terms of gross domestic product per capita (current prices, measured in U.S. dollars), as of April 2019. See International Monetary Fund, "IMF DataMapper: GDP Per Capita, Current Prices," webpage, undated. More broadly regarding economic conditions in Afghanistan, see World Bank, "The World Bank in Afghanistan: Overview," webpage, last updated October 13, 2019.

References: Peace Agreements and Related Documents

Agreement Between the Government of the Islamic Republic of Pakistan, the Government of the Islamic Republic of Afghanistan, and the United Nations High Commissioner for Refugees Governing the Repatriation of Afghan Citizens Living in Pakistan, Islamabad, Pakistan, August 2, 2007.

Agreement on a Comprehensive Political Settlement of the Cambodia Conflict ("Paris Peace Agreements"), Paris, October 23, 1991.

Agreement on Provisional Arrangements in Afghanistan Pending the Re-Establishment of Permanent Government Institutions ("Bonn Agreement"), Bonn, Germany, December 5, 2001.

Agreement Reached in the Multi-Party Negotiations ("Good Friday Agreement" or "Belfast Agreement"), Belfast, United Kingdom, April 10, 1998.

Argentina, Australia, Belgium, et al., Treaty of Peace with Japan, San Francisco, Calif., September 8, 1951.

Declaration of the Tashkent Conference on Afghanistan: Peace Process, Security Cooperation and Regional Connectivity, Tashkent, Uzbekistan, March 30, 2018.

Document of National Accord ("Taif Accords"), Taif, Saudi Arabia, October 22, 1989.

Final Declaration of the Geneva Conference on the Problem of Restoring Peace in Indo-China, Geneva, Switzerland, July 21, 1954.

Government of the Arab Republic of Egypt and Government of the State of Israel, Peace Treaty Between Israel and Egypt, Washington, D.C., March 26, 1979.

Government of Burundi et al., Arusha Peace and Reconciliation Agreement for Burundi ("Burundian Arusha Accords"), Arusha, Tanzania, August 28, 2000.

Government of the Central African Republic et al., Global Peace Agreement, Libreville, Gabon, June 21, 2008.

Government of Colombia and Revolutionary Armed Forces of Colombia, Agreement on Victims of the Conflict: "Comprehensive System of Truth, Justice, Reparation and Non-Repetition," Including the Special Jurisdiction for Peace; and Commitment on Human Rights, Havana, Cuba, December 15, 2015.

———, Final Agreement to End the Armed Conflict and Build a Stable and Lasting Peace, Bogota, Colombia, November 24, 2016.

Government of Croatia and Serb Negotiating Delegation, Basic Agreement on the Region of Eastern Slavonia, Baranja and Western Sirmium ("Erdut Agreement"), Erdut, Croatia, and Zagreb, Croatia, November 12, 1995.

Government of the Democratic Republic of the Congo and the Congrès National pour la Défense du Peuple (CNDP), Peace Agreement, Goma, Democratic Republic of Congo, March 23, 2009.

Government of El Salvador and Farabundo Martí National Liberation Front, Chapultepec Peace Agreement, Mexico City, Mexico, January 16, 1992.

Government of the French Republic and the Algerian National Liberation Front, Évian Accords, Évian, France, March 18, 1962.

Government of Guinea-Bissau and the Self-Proclaimed Military Junta, Agreement Between the Government of Guinea-Bissau and the Self-Proclaimed Military Junta ("Abuja Peace Agreement"), Abuja, Nigeria, November 1, 1998.

Government of the Islamic Republic of Afghanistan, "Offering Peace: Framing the Kabul Conference of February 28, 2018," February 28, 2018.

Government of the Islamic Republic of Afghanistan and Government of the Islamic Republic of Pakistan, Afghanistan-Pakistan Transit Trade Agreement, Kabul, Afghanistan, October 28, 2010.

Government of the Islamic Republic of Afghanistan and Hizb-e Islami of Afghanistan, Agreement, Kabul, Afghanistan, September 22, 2016.

Government of Nepal and Communist Party of Nepal (Maoist), Comprehensive Peace Accord, Kathmandu, Nepal, November 21, 2006.

Government of Papua New Guinea and Bougainville Interim Government, Lincoln Agreement on Peace Security and Development on Bougainville, Lincoln, New Zealand, January 23, 1998.

Government of Papua New Guinea and Bougainville Interim Provincial Government, Bougainville Peace Agreement, Arawa, Bougainville, Papua New Guinea, August 30, 2001.

Government of the People's Republic of Angola and Government of the Republic of Cuba, Agreement on the Conclusions of the Internationalist Mission of the Cuban Military Contingent, New York, December 22, 1988.

Government of the People's Republic of Angola, Government of the Republic of Cuba, and Government of the Republic of South Africa, Protocol of Geneva, Geneva, Switzerland, August 5, 1988.

Government of the People's Republic of Angola and the National Union for the Total Independence of Angola, Peace Accords for Angola ("Bicesse Accords"), Lisbon, Portugal, May 31, 1991.

Government of the Philippines and the Moro Islamic Liberation Front, Annex on Normalization to the Framework Agreement on the Bangsamaro (FAB), Kuala Lumpur, Malaysia, January 25, 2014.

Government of the Republic of Angola and the Cabinda Forum for Dialogue, Memorandum of Understanding for Peace and Reconciliation of the Province of Cabinda, Namibe, Angola, August 1, 2006.

Government of the Republic of Angola and the National Union for the Total Independence of Angola (UNITA), Lusaka Protocol, Lusaka, Zambia, November 15, 1994.

———, Memorandum of Understanding ("Luena Agreement"), Luena, Angola, April 4, 2002.

Government of the Republic of Djibouti and Front for the Restoration of Unity and Democracy, Agreement for Reform and Civil Concord, Djibouti, February 7, 2000.

Government of the Republic of Indonesia and the Free Aceh Movement, Cessation of Hostilities Framework Agreement, December 9, 2002.

Government of the Republic of Liberia, Liberians United for Reconciliation and Democracy, and Movement for Democracy in Liberia, Accra Comprehensive Peace Agreement, Accra, Ghana, August 18, 2003.

Government of the Republic of Mali et al., Agreement for Peace and Reconciliation in Mali Resulting from the Algiers Process, Bamako, Mali, May 15, 2015.

Government of the Republic of the Philippines and the Moro National Liberation Front, The Final Agreement on the Implementation of the 1976 Tripoli Agreement Between the Government of the Republic of the Philippines and the Moro National Liberation Front ("Mindanao Final Agreement"), Manila, Philippines, September 2, 1996.

Government of the Republic of Rwanda and the Rwandese Patriotic Front, N'sele Ceasefire Agreement, Arusha, Tanzania, July 12, 1992.

———, Protocol of Agreement on the Repatriation of Rwandese Refugees and the Resettlement of Displaced Persons, Arusha, Tanzania, June 9, 1993a.

———, Peace Agreement Between the Government of the Republic of Rwanda and the Rwandese Patriotic Front ("Rwandan Arusha Accords"), Arusha, Tanzania, August 4, 1993b.

Government of the Republic of the Sudan and Sudan People's Liberation Movement/Sudan People's Liberation Army, The Comprehensive Peace Agreement, Naivasha, Kenya, January 9, 2005.

Government of the Republic of the Union of Myanmar and the Ethnic Armed Organizations, The Nationwide Ceasefire Agreement, Naypyidaw, Myanmar, October 15, 2015.

Government of Sierra Leone and the Revolutionary United Front of Sierra Leone, Peace Agreement Between the Government of the Republic of Sierra Leone and the Revolutionary United Front of Sierra Leone ("Abidjan Accords"), Abidjan, Côte d'Ivoire, November 30, 1996.

———, Peace Agreement Between the Government of Sierra Leone and the Revolutionary United Front of Sierra Leone ("Lomé Peace Agreement"), Lomé, Togo, July 7, 1999.

Government of Sudan, South Sudan United Democratic Salvation Front, et al., The Sudan Peace Agreement ("Khartoum Peace Agreement"), Khartoum, Sudan, April 21, 1997.

Government of Tajikistan and United Tajik Opposition, Protocol on the Main Functions and Powers of the Commission on National Reconciliation, Moscow, Russia, December 23, 1996a.

———, Statute of the Commission on National Reconciliation, Moscow, Russia, December 23, 1996b.

———, Protocol on Political Questions, Bishkek, Kyrgyzstan, May 18, 1997a.

———, Protocol on the Guarantees of Implementation of the General Agreement on Establishment of Peace and National Accord in Tajikistan, Tehran, Iran, May 28, 1997b.

Heart of Asia-Istanbul Process: Deepening Cooperation for Sustainable Security and Prosperity of the 'Heart of Asia' Region, Beijing, China, October 31, 2014.

Interim Agreement for Peace and Self-Government in Kosovo ("Rambouillet Agreement"), Rambouillet, France, February 23, 1999.

Islamic State of Afghanistan, Hizb-e Islami, et al., Afghan Peace Accord ("Islamabad Accord"), Islamabad, Pakistan, March 7, 1993.

National Unity Government of the Islamic Republic of Afghanistan et al., Afghanistan and International Community: Commitments to Reforms and Renewed Partnership, London, December 4, 2014.

Pakistan, Swat Peace Accord, February 16, 2009.

People's Republic of Angola, Republic of Cuba, and Republic of South Africa, Agreement Among the People's Republic of Angola, the Republic of Cuba, and the Republic of South Africa ("Tripartite Agreement"), New York, December 22, 1988.

People's Republic of Bangladesh and United People's Party of the Chittagong Hill Tracts, Chittagong Hill Tracts Peace Accord, Dhaka, Bangladesh, December 2, 1997.

Peshawar Accord, Peshawar, Pakistan, April 24, 1992.

Republic of Afghanistan and Islamic Republic of Pakistan, Bilateral Agreement Between the Republic of Afghanistan and the Islamic Republic of Pakistan on the Principles of Mutual Relations, in Particular on Non-Interference and Non-Intervention, Geneva, Switzerland, April 14, 1988a.

———, Agreement on the Interrelationships for the Settlement of the Situation Relating to Afghanistan, Geneva, Switzerland, April 14, 1988b.

Republic of Afghanistan, Islamic Republic of Pakistan, Union of Soviet Socialist Republics, and United States of America, Agreements on the Settlement of the Situation Relating to Afghanistan ("Geneva Accords"), Geneva, Switzerland, April 14, 1988.

Republic of Bosnia and Herzegovina, Republic of Croatia, and Federal Republic of Yugoslavia, General Framework Agreement for Peace in Bosnia and Herzegovina ("Dayton Agreement"), Paris, France, December 14, 1995.

Republic of Burundi, Constitution, March 18, 2005.

Republic of Côte d'Ivoire and Forces Nouvelles de Côte d'Ivoire, Ouagadougou Political Agreement, Ouagadougou, Burkina Faso, March 4, 2007.

Republic of Macedonia, Internal Macedonian Revolutionary Organization – Democratic Party for Macedonian National Unity, Democratic Party of Albanians, Social Democratic Union of Macedonia, and Party for Democratic Prosperity, Framework Agreement ("Ohrid Agreement"), Ohrid, Macedonia, August 13, 2001.

Republic of Mozambique and RENAMO, General Peace Agreement for Mozambique ("Rome Accords"), Rome, Italy, October 4, 1992.

Republic of South Africa, Constitution of 1993 ("Interim Constitution"), Act No. 200 of 1993, January 24, 1994.

Republic of South Sudan and Sudan People's Liberation Movement-in-Opposition, Agreement on the Resolution of the Conflict in the Republic of South Sudan, Addis Ababa, Ethiopia, August 17, 2015.

Stormont House Agreement, Belfast, Northern Ireland, December 23, 2014.

Transitional Administration of Afghanistan and the Governments of China, the Islamic Republic of Iran, Pakistan, Tajikistan, Turkmenistan, and Uzbekistan, Kabul Declaration on Good-Neighbourly Relations, Kabul, Afghanistan, December 22, 2002.

Transitional Government of Burundi and the Conseil National pour la Défense de la Démocratie-Forces pour la Défense de la Démocratie, Ceasefire Agreement, Arusha, Tanzania, December 2, 2002.

Union of Soviet Socialist Republics, United Kingdom of Great Britain and Northern Ireland, United States of America, France, and Austria, State Treaty for the Re-Establishment of an Independent and Democratic Austria, Vienna, Austria, May 15, 1955.

United States of America, Democratic Republic of Vietnam, Provisional Revolutionary Government of South Vietnam, and Republic of Vietnam, Agreement on Ending the War and Restoring Peace in Viet Nam ("Paris Peace Accords"), Paris, France, January 27, 1973.

United States of America and the Republic of Iraq, Agreement on the Withdrawal of United States Forces from Iraq and the Organization of Their Activities During Their Temporary Presence in Iraq ("U.S.–Iraq Status of Forces Agreement"), Baghdad, Iraq, November 17, 2008a.

———, Strategic Framework Agreement for a Relationship of Friendship and Cooperation, Baghdad, Iraq, November 17, 2008b.

References: Secondary Sources

Andisha, Nasir A., "Neutrality in Afghanistan's Foreign Policy," Washington, D.C.: U.S. Institute of Peace, March 2015.

Barfield, Thomas, "Afghanistan's Political History: Prospects for Peaceful Opposition," *Accord*, No. 27, June 2018.

Bell, Christine, Rachel Anderson, Sanja Badanjak, Robert Forster, Astrid Jamar, Jan Pospisil, and Laura Wise, *Peace Agreements Database and Dataset Codebook*, Version 1, Edinburgh, Scotland: University of Edinburgh, February 19, 2018.

Bell, Christine, and Sanja Badanjak, "Introducing PA-X: A New Peace Agreement Database and Dataset," *Journal of Peace Research*, Vol. 56, No. 3, 2019, pp. 452–466.

Bell, Christine, and Kimana Zulueta-Fülscher, *Sequencing Peace Agreements and Constitutions in the Political Settlement Process*, Stockholm, Sweden: International IDEA, November 2016.

Brandt, Michele, Jill Cottrell, Yash Ghai, and Anthony Regan, *Constitution-Making and Reform: Options for the Process*, Geneva, Switzerland: Interpeace, November 2011.

Cammett, Melani, and Edmund Malesky, "Power Sharing in Postconflict Societies: Implications for Peace and Governance," *Journal of Conflict Resolution*, Vol. 56, No. 6, 2012, pp. 982–1016.

Caspersen, Nina, *Peace Agreements: Finding Solutions to Intra-State Conflicts*, Cambridge, United Kingdom: Polity Press, 2017.

Cederman, Lars-Erik, Andreas Wimmer, and Brian Min, "Why Do Ethnic Groups Rebel?: New Data and Analysis," *World Politics*, Vol. 62, No. 1, January 2010, pp. 87–119.

Derouen, Karl, Jr., Jenna Lea, and Peter Wallensteen, "The Duration of Civil War Peace Agreements," *Conflict Management and Peace Science*, Vol. 26, No. 4, September 2009, pp. 367–387.

Deschamps, Colin, and Alan Roe, *Land Conflict in Afghanistan: Building Capacity to Address Vulnerability*, Kabul, Afghanistan: Afghanistan Research and Evaluation Unit, April 2009.

Displacement Solutions and Norwegian Refugee Council, *Housing, Land and Property Rights and Peace Agreements: Guidance for the Myanmar Peace Process*, February 2018.

Dobbins, James, Jason H. Campbell, Sean Mann, and Laurel E. Miller, *Consequences of a Precipitous Withdrawal from Afghanistan*, Santa Monica, Calif.: RAND Corporation, PE-326-RC, 2019. As of October 3, 2019: https://www.rand.org/pubs/perspectives/PE326.html

Gaston, Erica, and Lilian Dang, "Addressing Land Conflict in Afghanistan," Washington, D.C.: U.S. Institute of Peace, June 2015.

Giustozzi, Antonio, *Negotiating with the Taliban: Issues and Prospects*, New York: Century Foundation, 2010.

Giustozzi, Antonio, Claudio Franco, and Adam Baczko, *Shadow Justice: How the Taliban Run Their Judiciary*, Kabul, Afghanistan: Integrity Watch Afghanistan, 2013.

Grossman, Marc, "Talking to the Taliban 2011–2012: A Reflection," *Prism*, Vol. 4, No. 4, 2014, pp. 21–37.

Harpviken, Kristian Berg, and Shahrbanou Tadjbakhsh, *A Rock Between Hard Places: Afghanistan as an Arena of Regional Insecurity*, New York: Oxford University Press, 2016.

Hartzell, Caroline A., "Mixed Motives? Explaining the Decision to Integrate Militaries at Civil War's End," in Roy Licklider, ed., *New Armies from Old: Merging Competing Military Forces After Civil Wars*, Washington, D.C.: Georgetown University Press, 2014, pp. 13–28.

Hartzell, Caroline A., and Matthew Hoddie, "Institutionalizing Peace: Power Sharing and Post-Civil War Conflict Management," *American Journal of Political Science*, Vol. 47, No. 2, April 2003, pp. 318–332.

———, *Crafting Peace: Power-Sharing Institutions and the Negotiated Settlement of Civil Wars*, University Park, Pa.: Penn State University Press, 2007.

———, "The Art of the Possible: Power Sharing and Post–Civil War Democracy," *World Politics*, Vol. 67, No. 1, January 2015, pp. 37–71.

Horowitz, Donald L., *Ethnic Groups in Conflict*, Berkeley, Calif.: University of California Press, 1985.

International Monetary Fund, "IMF DataMapper: GDP Per Capita, Current Prices," webpage, undated. As of October 17, 2019: https://www.imf.org/external/datamapper/NGDPDPC@WEO/USA/DEU/SSD

Jackson, Ashley, *Life Under the Taliban Shadow Government*, London: Overseas Development Institute, June 2018.

Joshi, Madhav, and John Darby, "Introducing the Peace Accords Matrix (PAM): A Database of Comprehensive Peace Agreements and Their Implementation, 1989–2007," *Peacebuilding*, Vol. 1, No. 2, 2013, pp. 256–274.

Joshi, Madhav, SungYong Lee, and Roger Mac Ginty, "Built-In Safeguards and the Implementation of Civil War Peace Accords," *International Interactions*, Vol. 43, No. 6, 2017, pp. 994–1018.

Joshi, Madhav, and Jason Michael Quinn, "Is the Sum Greater than the Parts? The Terms of Civil War Peace Agreements and the Commitment Problem Revisited," *Negotiation Journal*, Vol. 31, No. 1, January 2015a, pp. 7–30.

———, *Peace Accords Matrix Implementation Dataset (PAM_ID) Codebook*, Version 1.5, Notre Dame, Ind.: Kroc Institute for International Peace Studies, updated July 29, 2015b. As of October 16, 2019:
https://peaceaccords.nd.edu/sites/default/files/PAM_ID%20CODEBOOK%20V.1.5%2029July2015.pdf

———, "Implementing the Peace: The Aggregate Implementation of Comprehensive Peace Agreements and Peace Duration After Intrastate Armed Conflict," *British Journal of Political Science*, Vol. 47, No. 4, October 2017, pp. 869–892.

Joshi, Madhav, Jason Michael Quinn, and Patrick M. Regan, "Annualized Implementation Data on Comprehensive Intrastate Peace Accords, 1989–2012," *Journal of Peace Research*, Vol. 52, No. 4, 2015, pp. 551–562.

Kane, Sean, "Talking with the Taliban: Should the Afghan Constitution Be a Point of Negotiation?" Washington, D.C.: U.S. Institute of Peace, January 2015.

Kishi, Roudabeh, and Melissa Pavlik, *ACLED 2018: The Year in Review*, Madison, Wisc.: Armed Conflict Location and Event Data Project, January 11, 2019. As of October 3, 2019:
https://www.acleddata.com/2019/01/11/acled-2018-the-year-in-review/

Krebs, Ronald R., and Roy Licklider, "United They Fall: Why the International Community Should Not Promote Military Integration After Civil War," *International Security*, Vol. 40, No. 3, Winter 2015/2016, pp. 93–138.

Kroc Institute for International Peace Studies, "Peace Accords Matrix," webpage, 2015. As of October 16, 2019:
https://peaceaccords.nd.edu

Larson, Anna, and Alexander Ramsbotham, eds., "Incremental Peace in Afghanistan," *Accord*, No. 27, June 2018 (entire issue).

Lauterpacht Centre for International Law, "Language of Peace," Legal Tools for Peace-Making Project, Cambridge, United Kingdom: University of Cambridge, 2018. As of December 6, 2018:
https://www.languageofpeace.org/

Lijphart, Arend, *Democracy in Plural Societies: A Comparative Exploration*, New Haven, Conn.: Yale University Press, 1977.

Mashal, Mujib, "What Do the Taliban Want in Afghanistan? A Lost Constitution Offers Clues," *New York Times*, June 28, 2019.

Matanock, Aila M., "Bullets for Ballots: Electoral Participation Provisions and Enduring Peace After Civil Conflict," *International Security*, Vol. 41, No. 4, Spring 2017, pp. 93–132.

Mattes, Michaela, and Burcu Savun, "Fostering Peace After Civil War: Commitment Problems and Agreement Design," *International Studies Quarterly*, Vol. 53, No. 3, September 2009, pp. 737–759.

———, "Information, Agreement Design, and the Durability of Civil War Settlements," *American Journal of Political Science*, Vol. 54, No. 2, April 2010, pp. 511–524.

Miller, Laurel E., "Designing Constitution-Making Processes: Lessons from the Past, Questions for the Future," in Laurel E. Miller, ed., *Framing the State in Times of Transition: Case Studies in Constitution Making*, Washington, D.C.: U.S. Institute of Peace Press, 2010, pp. 601–665.

Miller, Laurel, and Graeme Smith, "Behind Trump's Taliban Debacle," International Crisis Group, September 10, 2019. As of November 6, 2019:
https://www.crisisgroup.org/asia/south-asia/afghanistan/behind-trumps-taliban-debacle

Najafizada, Eltaf, and Chris Kay, "Ghani Says Afghanistan Hit by 'Undeclared War' from Pakistan," Bloomberg, June 6, 2017. As of October 4, 2019:
https://www.bloomberg.com/news/articles/2017-06-06/ghani-says-afghanistan-suffering-undeclared-war-from-pakistan

Osman, Borhan, *A Negotiated End to the Afghan Conflict: The Taliban's Perspective*, Washington, D.C.: U.S. Institute of Peace, 2018.

Osman, Borhan, and Anand Gopal, *Taliban Views on a Future State*, New York: New York University Center on International Cooperation, July 2016.

PA-X, *Peace Agreements Database and Access Tool, Version 1*, Edinburgh, Scotland: Political Settlements Research Programme, University of Edinburgh, 2017. As of February 6, 2019:
https://www.peaceagreements.org/

Price, Gareth, "Afghanistan and Its Neighbours: Forging Regional Engagement," London: Chatham House, May 2015. As of October 14, 2019: https://www.chathamhouse.org/publication/afghanistan-and-its-neighbours-forging-regional-engagement

Roessler, Philip, and David Ohls, "Self-Enforcing Power Sharing in Weak States," *International Organization*, Vol. 72, No. 2, Spring 2018, pp. 423–454.

Rothchild, Donald, and Philip G. Roeder, "Power Sharing as an Impediment to Peace and Democracy," in Philip G. Roeder and Donald Rothchild, eds., *Sustainable Peace: Power and Democracy After Civil Wars*, Ithaca, N.Y.: Cornell University Press, 2005, pp. 29–50.

Rubin, Barnett R., "Everyone Wants a Piece of Afghanistan," *Foreign Policy*, March 11, 2019.

Shinn, James, and James Dobbins, *Afghan Peace Talks: A Primer*, Santa Monica, Calif.: RAND Corporation, MG-1131-RC, 2011. As of October 3, 2019: https://www.rand.org/pubs/monographs/MG1131.html

Snyder, Jack, and Leslie Vinjamuri, "Trials and Errors: Principle and Pragmatism in Strategies of International Justice," *International Security*, Vol. 28, No. 3, Winter 2003/2004, pp. 5–44.

Thier, J. Alexander, "Big Tent, Small Tent: The Making of a Constitution in Afghanistan," in Laurel E. Miller, ed., *Framing the State in Times of Transition: Case Studies in Constitution Making*, Washington, D.C.: U.S. Institute of Peace Press, 2010, pp. 535–562.

Tomsen, Peter, *The Wars of Afghanistan: Messianic Terrorism, Tribal Conflicts, and the Failures of Great Powers*, New York: Public Affairs, 2011.

United Nations, "Peace Agreements Database Search," webpage, undated. As of February 6, 2019:
https://peacemaker.un.org/document-search

United Nations Security Council, "Procedures for Delisting," webpage, undated. As of October 15, 2019:
https://www.un.org/securitycouncil/sanctions/1267/aq_sanctions_list/procedures-for-delisting

University of Edinburgh, "Peace Agreements Database," webpage, undated. As of October 16, 2019:
https://www.peaceagreements.org

U.S. Department of State, "Remarks at the Launch of the Asia Society's Series of Richard C. Holbrooke Memorial Address," February 18, 2011. As of October 4, 2019:
https://2009-2017.state.gov/secretary/20092013clinton/rm/2011/02/156815.htm

Vinjamuri, Leslie, "The Distant Promise of a Negotiated Justice," *Daedalus*, Vol. 146, No. 1, Winter 2017, pp. 100–112.

Vinjamuri, Leslie, and Aaron P. Boesenecker, *Accountability and Peace Agreements: Mapping Trends from 1980 to 2006*, Geneva, Switzerland: Centre for Humanitarian Dialogue, September 2007.

Voice of Jihad, "Transcript of Speech Delivered by Delegation of Islamic Emirate at Moscow Conference," November 9, 2018. As of February 6, 2019: https://alemarahenglish.com/?p=37316

Walter, Barbara F., *Committing to Peace: The Successful Settlement of Civil Wars*, Princeton, N.J.: Princeton University Press, 2002.

White House, "Remarks by President Trump on the Strategy in Afghanistan and South Asia," August 21, 2017. As of October 4, 2019: https://www.whitehouse.gov/briefings-statements/remarks-president-trump-strategy-afghanistan-south-asia/

World Bank, "The World Bank in Afghanistan: Overview," webpage, last updated October 13, 2019. As of October 17, 2019: https://www.worldbank.org/en/country/afghanistan/overview

Yusuf, Moeed, Huma Yusuf, and Salman Zaidi, "Pakistan, the United States and the End Game in Afghanistan: Perceptions of Pakistan's Foreign Policy Elite," Washington, D.C.: U.S. Institute of Peace, July 25, 2011.